One Way Single

Sheila Stevens

Dianthus Publishing

Published by Dianthus Publishing Limited,
The Pool House,
Kemble · Cirencester. GL7 6AD
Tel. 01285 770 239   Fax: 01285 770 896
e-mail: cbrann @ dianthus.prestel.co.uk
Printed in Europe by the Alden Group, Oxford

© Sheila Stevens, 2001, **ISBN 0-946604-21-5**
The song 'Faithful One' by Brian DDoerksen © 1989 Mercy/VineyardPublishing, P.O.Box 68025, Anaheim, CA 92817-0825.USA www.vineyardmusic.com

Illustrations:

CONTENTS

To my parents, William Geoffrey and Muriel Stevens, who gave me such a wonderful start in life and never once gave me cause to doubt their love for me

by the Rt. Rev. John Perry, Bishop of Chelmsford

As readers will discover, Sheila Stevens was a member of the Lee Abbey Community in Devon during the time that I was the Warden, so I read *One Way Single* with special interest and curiosity. Would it match the person I knew and held in high regard? I was not disappointed. In fact, it makes compelling reading.

With refreshing honesty and humour, and writing with a beautifully clear and concise style, the author charts her journey through life, holding nothing back. From start to finish, her story has an authentic ring about it. What Sheila has written is what she is.

Single or married, you will find much here to glean and learn from, as well as to smile about. Throughout, you will discern the unmistakable marks of the presence of the Lord whom Sheila has loved and gladly served over the years. In her 'ups and downs' she has experienced the friendship, healing and transforming grace of Jesus Christ. As a result, I believe her book will be an encouragement, challenge and blessing to many.

You are in for a treat. Read *One Way Single* and enjoy it to the full!

✝ John Perry

Bishop of Chelmsford

One Way - Single

Family pictures from my childhood:
Above, my mother Muriel with my father, myself (l) and brother Michael (r)
Below, Betty's brother George (l) and brother Michael with myself (l) and Betty (r)

The Journey Begins

I was born on 7 June 1919 in Preesall, a small village near Fleetwood in Lancashire where my father a Civil Engineer was manager of a salt mine. I learned years later that my mother was very fearful during the pregnancy at the thought of bringing another child into a home where there were increasing tensions in the marriage. Maybe some of that anxiety was transmitted to me as she told me I came into the world like a frightened rabbit!

We had moved to Cleveleys when I became conscious that I was alive. Certainly the picture I have of myself then is not of a scared rabbit but a little girl who could sit still happily with a book and was also full of energy and enthusiasm whose motto was 'what shall I/we do next?' One of my happiest memories is of a Sunday afternoon when four or five of us children would pile into the back of our open-top Standard car and go to Littledale, our favourite picnic place in the Trough of Bowland, a perfect area for climbing around outcrops of rock, where we could get rid of surplus energy. The drive there was equally exciting for children and adults. We were either watching eagerly for the ice-cream man on his tricycle or hanging over the back of the car blowing kisses to the occupants of passing cars. The only condition was that if there was no response to our wave there would be no kiss. These were very carefree days with wonderful memories of the freedom Michael my brother and I enjoyed in our childhood.

Michael was 4 years older and I both idolised and envied him. I would rather have been a boy; he could wear trousers and go to bed late! I do not think I was a tomboy, I preferred playing with my dolls and stuffed toys rather than with soldiers and trains, but I clearly remember shuffling around the kitchen in my father's big shoes, with his cap on my head, hearing my mother's 'help' exclaim in broad Lancashire "Ee-ee Mrs Stevens, you'll never make a lady of 'er"!

Children seemed to gravitate to our house and garden; we were fortunate to have so many friends. My best friend was Betty Wadsworth (now Sonley). We spent hours playing, chattering and giggling together. We were, and still are, like sisters – though not quite so giggly now!

Fun, games, picnics and parties loom very large in my memory. We had the sea and the countryside on our doorstep and we had lovely holidays in the Lake District and Yorkshire. We were privileged children.

Sunday was always a special day. To start with when the church bells rang at 8.00 am I was allowed to read and eat a little bowl of goodies that was always by my bed on a Sunday morning.

Both my parents had a Christian background. My grandfather and uncle on my mother's side were Congregational Ministers and my father had four aunts who were all missionaries. My parents took my brother and me to the Congregational Church in Cleveleys. My chief recollection is of being kept quiet by opening and shutting the fox's mouth on the end of my mother's fur stole; it seemed an endless fun occupation. At the same time I recall that I was introduced to Jesus in the children's sermons that I loved, and also in our goodnight prayers.

My mother said she learned a spiritual lesson when she gently rebuked Michael for his extended prayer:– 'God bless Mummy, God bless Daddy, God bless Sheila, God bless the armchair, God bless the carpet, God bless the gas stove . . .' when challenged he said 'I think God likes a good laugh'. I think she agreed! Good spiritual seeds were sown in my childhood.

I look back with gratitude for the wonderfully secure start my parents gave me in life; I owe them a great deal. They were two such fine people but with very different personalities and expectations of life. My father was a quiet, very private man, not given to showing his emotions, a mine of general knowledge with a nice sense of humour. He was perfectly happy to spend the whole day on his own in the garden or in the shed making things of wood. My mother on the other hand was outgoing, a people person, socially gifted with a vivid personality and a keen sense of humour.

Sadly the differences in personality together with very dissimilar interests did not help their marriage, but I believe the main trouble came when my mother discovered, much against her will, that if she did not take responsibility and make decisions in the important areas, socially, domestically and as far as we children were concerned, no decisions would be made. If they could have talked it out, things might have been different, but as it was they stayed together increasingly pursuing their own interests. I loved both my parents but my relationship with them was completely different, and for me it was their very differences that gave me such a happy childhood, and not only the best start in life but much that would continue with me throughout my journey. As I think of my interests today I recognise their origin in my early childhood. My father taught me how to use a camera and take a photograph. I even remember helping him develop films and still have some of the sepia prints we produced.

I spent many hours under his guidance colouring in heraldic shields, which I am sure sparked off the enjoyment of drawing and painting which I have had over the years. He taught my brother and me to row a boat and took us walking in the mountains. I still love boats, without oars, and I still love mountains, without the walking. My relationship with my father was very much through shared interests rather than anything more personal.

My mother was the one who could enter into the mind of a child and know instinctively how to respond whether it was 'Mummy, what shall I do next?' or when from the top of the stairs after bedtime a little voice cried 'Mummy I've got earache.' She knew I was really saying 'Please come I want to know you are still here.' I loved my mother reading to us by the fire or playing the piano for us to sing to. Reading and music have always been an essential part of my life. I could talk to my mother about anything and she was the one I would go to with my tears and little worries. She would battle for anything she considered best for my brother and me regardless of the cost to herself.

This unselfish love was the greatest contribution she could have made to my journey, she was certainly the major influence in terms of my mental and emotional stability. Without her wisdom and persistence my story would have been very different. I doubt if I would have gone to boarding school or even had a career.

My mother told me later in life that the reason she wanted boarding school for me was that I was getting too dependent on her. I believe she could also see that I was becoming aware that all was not well in the home and, at least in term time, I would be out of the atmosphere of tension. I have no recollection of being told I was going away to school or of my reactions.

I know that the Burgess Hill School for Girls in Sussex was carefully chosen so that I could be close to some of the family. My grandparents, uncle and aunt, and three great-aunts on my father's side, all lived near the school and had homes for me to visit when I was allowed out.

Boarding School

In September 1929 at the age of 10 I began the next stage in my journey.– boarding school. My first two or three terms were not happy ones. I think leaving home was a traumatic experience. I arrived at school feeling very shy and insecure and became a prime target for teasing.

I remember one very painful incident when for no apparent reason I was 'sent to Coventry' for two or three days and no one would speak to me. Thirty years later God brought this incident back to my mind when I was finding it difficult to contribute in group discussion: if a remark of mine was ignored I would retreat into silence. This highlighted for me how even a small incident from the past can have such damaging repercussions. Fortunately, I was able to talk and pray things through with a friend and find healing.

After the initial unhappiness, my natural enthusiasm soon came to the fore and I entered into every aspect of school life with zest and made many friends. Being an active child I preferred sport to lessons and enjoyed the extra-curricular activities – apart from one! Even in this I have to see God's hand.

I loved singing and was an enthusiastic member of the school choir under the direction of Miss Meriel Green, a professional singer. I begged my mother to let me have singing lessons and she, discerning that my enthusiasm rather out-weighed my talent, wisely said, 'Yes, if Miss Green considers your voice worth training.' Unfortunately my teacher did not see me as a budding Maria Callas and instead of singing I found myself having elocution lessons. I was not pleased. In retrospect, I am quite sure the voice training I received then was a help when I started speaking in public 45 years later.

This was not the only seed sown for the future. I can see now that as games captain and head of the school seeds of leadership were sown that would bear fruit in years to come.

Church going at school was compulsory and it was the only day when we could discard school uniform and wear our own dresses and, of course in those days, a hat. I can see mine now, a bright red concoction, which for some reason had been made for me. I think it was more embarrassing than beautifying!

Every now and again I was allowed to go to the Congregational Church with my three ex-missionary great aunts who lived next door to the school. I do not think I enjoyed that very much but I did appreciate their delicious Sunday afternoon teas as I did when I visited my other relatives who lived near and had me out regularly.

Normally on Sundays we alternated by going to two different Anglican churches. The first a 'low' church where, to my recollection, the Vicar preached mainly on cricket and was therefore boring. The second an Anglo-Catholic church where, as I got older, I would go happily to the compulsory morning and optional evening services because I was 'in love' with the tall dark and handsome Vicar!

I made a very impressive collection of his signatures from the church magazine and was first on the list when he came up to the school to meet any girl who would like a private chat. I think the headmistress smelled a rat when I

Head girl at Burgess Hill

headed the list for the second time. My request was not granted!

When I was 12 my parents moved to Prenton outside Birkenhead and it was there I was baptised before being confirmed at school. I was fortunate in being prepared for both these events by two dear godly men who taught me well about the Christian faith.

I remember my actual confirmation day very well because it was the custom in those days for candidates to wear white. All we had were our tennis dresses, which were not exactly becoming for the occasion. In spite of this I took the service very seriously. I am not sure how much I understood or how real it was but I am certain a few more bricks were added to the good foundation I had received at home.

Apart from churchgoing and confirmation we did have regular RE lessons. I can also remember pacing up and down a corridor trying to get a psalm into my head. I cannot recall if this was for a spiritual exercise or punishment. For me it was probably punishment as I found memorizing anything extremely difficult. I cannot recall that we had any sex education at school in the 1930s but I must have learned some of the facts of life at least before I was twelve as the following story proves.

In the summer terms we were allowed to keep small pets as long as they were males. Of course my guinea pig called Nibble decided she was female and produced two babies! I was mortified at being accused of not reporting them, the gardener would not believe that guinea pigs were born with fur which I knew to be true. After a tremendous fuss the babies were banished to a foster home and I was allowed to keep Nibble for the rest of the term providing she did not fall from grace again. I wrote home very scornful of their ignorance saying 'How could Nibble have any more babies when she does not have a man!'

I have to mention holidays which were a very important part of school. I was always excited at the thought of going home but experienced a real mixture of happy times and a growing feeling of paralysis inside, finding it difficult to respond with natural affection to my parents. Thankfully I never failed to keep a good relationship with both of them. Our little wirehaired terrier Tinker lapped up my affections and was also a very good listener!

Holidays produced another problem: becoming increasingly aware of a body which I did not like very much. I was tall for my age and not exactly sylphlike and so shopping for clothes was a nightmare. I remember my mother dragging me to a dressmaker and standing in a silent sulk while she pinned me all over! It was many years before I could accept my body as God had made it. It was a heavy burden on my journey.

I hated returning to school after the holidays but a few minutes after rejoining my friends on the school train I closed the lid on the pain and was laughing. My mother, I know, walked back along the platform crying; it was costly for her. The more I think of my school days the more I thank my mother for her wisdom and unselfishness in sending me to the right school at the right time. It was a wonderful preparation for my next stage.

I think it became fairly obvious on the road so far that I would be more suited to a practical career rather than an academic one. I struggled with exams and was not interested or likely to get into University. Careers for women were limited before the Second World War and I have often been asked why I chose physiotherapy. The answer is I do not know; possibly because it was the most active hands-orientated career I could find. I do know it was absolutely the right choice for me and in 1936 I started my training at the Middlesex Hospital in London – a new step along the road.

Training Days

I chose the Middlesex Hospital because it was there I had the best and most relaxed interview and I liked the atmosphere. I found it was not only an excellent hospital but its location right in the middle of London was a bonus.

At first I lived with several others from my training set in a nearby hostel where the only place to study was in one's bedroom. It was very small, very sparse and freezing cold. I was thankful I had been conditioned by a school dormitory where we had used our floor mats on the bed to try to keep warm.

Two of us often joined forces sitting at each end of the bed wrapped in eiderdowns trying to study muscle attachments on bones or the course of various nerves. The most welcome sound was a knock on the door with an offer of free tickets for a theatre. It did not take long for eiderdowns to be thrown off, an evening dress pulled on and then a quick get-away to the best seats in the theatre. I prided myself on never having refused an offer.

I loved London; it was an exciting place to live, with so much to do and enjoy even with little money. One of our chief delights after a free theatre was a four-penny fish cake with tomato sauce and a cup of coffee at Lyons Corner House, the Mecca for the ordinary man or woman.

I also thoroughly enjoyed the training particularly the interactions with patients. Etched on my memory are the enormously fat local Jewish ladies who revelled in being guinea pigs for the learning of our massage and exercise techniques (because of their size, more massage than exercise I think!) I became so absorbed in hospital life and all the new experiences I was having in London that, though I did

Sheila's 'set' of physiotherapy trainees at the Middlesex. – (Sheila 2ⁿᵈ from l. 3ʳᵈ row down)

not consciously reject God, I just forgot him. Apart from visiting Westminster Abbey and St Paul's Cathedral as places of interest, I do not remember ever going to a church service during my training days.

A few months before the completion of my training war was declared and we were immediately sent home. Suddenly to have a blackout was a unique experience. I travelled home on a train lit only with tiny blue lights, jam-packed with troops, standing room only. It did not help to have a drunken amorous sailor next to me, but fortunately rescue was near at hand. A soldier saw my predicament, dealt with the sailor and gave me his seat. Travelling during the war, even in daytime, was not easy.

After two or three weeks at home I was re-called back to London and finished my training before the intense bombing began. I was now a qualified physiotherapist with MCSP after my name, another milestone, so what next? I knew I had to have at least two years' experience as a physiotherapist before I would be accepted to go abroad by any of the armed forces. So unless I changed direction completely the only choice was to look for a job in my chosen career.

The family home had moved once again to Willaston, a village in the Wirral. I spent some weeks at home and while there searching for a job I joined the Home Guard, an interesting experience. I never managed to get a uniform but every Sunday morning I was on parade learning the drill or with a rifle at target practice. I think I qualified well for 'Mum's Army', but fortunately a job came up before any call into battle.

A War-time Career

The experiences of my first job were very mixed. Northampton was not a friendly town in those days. I cannot remember being invited into a single home in my eighteen months there but I had my first taste of landladies. Looking back I can laugh at my first lodgings. I appreciated the kindness and good food but I did not appreciate some of the pettiness, for example being rebuked by my landlady's husband for hanging the bath chain over the wrong tap and putting the telephone down the wrong way!

Neither was I too pleased to have the landlady's daughter as a chaperone when a boyfriend came to visit. My landlady did her best to get me to church but her style of Christianity did not attract me and I declined every invitation. I was much more interested in the theatre and in the troops rather than God and the church.

I did make a small contribution to the war effort by helping at a canteen for the troops two nights a week. It was fun but extremely busy, the frying pan was in constant use and the washing up endless; no dishwashers in those days. I can still smell myself as I rode home on my bicycle!

As far as the job was concerned it was certainly not the best in terms of work experience for a young physiotherapist but it had its lighter moments. With another physiotherapist I was seconded from Manfield Orthopaedic Hospital to work in various outlying clinics. We travelled in a car provided by the hospital carrying all our heavy equipment with us. It was not unusual for this ancient relic to break down, usually in the dark, in the rain, on the way home. Most certainly one of the clinics would not have stood up to the present day health and safety regulations. We treated our patients on hard trestle tables in a dark and dingy room at the back of a Salvation Army hall. Any hot water we needed had to be boiled on an ancient black stove. On Tuesday afternoons we worked to the accompaniment of the Salvation Army songsters complete with tambourines at full volume!

One way and another my career had not started well, the job experience was not good. I was lonely, I had been in three different lodgings and I wanted the comfort of home. It was a totally selfish choice but a reflection of the insecurity within, so when a job came up in Liverpool I moved back to the Wirral. It was a mistake for all concerned. In my desperation I had forgotten something. I loved and got on well with both my parents individually but before long I was experiencing once again the conflicting emotions of knowing on the one hand the love and security of both father and mother but on the other hand hating the tensions of living within the atmosphere of their unhappy marriage which brought to the surface the feelings I knew so well of being torn apart yet frozen inside.

The bombing had not yet started in Liverpool but I was travelling long hours to Alder Hey Hospital and the job was not really what I wanted. I could have volunteered to serve abroad at this stage having had my two years' experience but again there was conflict, the outer me longing to go, the inner me not daring to take the decision.

After eighteen months at home I was quick to move on when I was offered what was to be the best job of my career so far, in a military hospital in Chertsey in Surrey. Botleys Park (now called St Peter's) was the centre for all the research and first uses of penicillin. Working there as a physiotherapist amongst war casualties could not have been more exciting or rewarding. We had top class surgeons and an infinite variety of injuries and wounds to treat.

One of the positive aspects of war was that the face and ethos of physiotherapy changed forever. Instead of massage and exercise it became rehabilitation, giving a far greater challenge and interest.

Apart from physiotherapy life in a military hospital was stimulating: there were so many home grown entertainments, dances and concerts and pantomimes, involving patients as well as staff; this was another positive aspect of the war. But just when life seemed to be going smoothly for me with a job I loved, a pleasant bed-sitting room and many friends, the unexpected happened.

As a result of the heavy physical work my back gave out and I found myself in my own hospital having two operations, the second of which, a spinal fusion, kept me on a plaster bed for four months. Looking back years later, I realised that although a genuine congenital defect was diagnosed and much as I loved my job, a part of me was glad to escape from life. Physically it was frustrating to be trapped on my back unable to move, but mentally and emotionally it set me free from facing the inner conflicts and fear, to enjoy the attention and cosseting which inevitably came my way.

However, I could not escape forever and came out of hospital and convalescence to a rude awakening. The Orthopaedic surgeon who had performed the operations suggested a return to part-time work but the hospital authorities decided I had had too much time off and I was dismissed. This was a bitter blow which made me consider giving up this particular work altogether. I might have done so if I could have thought of any other equally interesting occupation.

The war had just ended, jobs were difficult to find, lodgings even more so. Eventually I found both. An agreeable enough part-time job in a physiotherapy clinic, but very disagreeable lodgings where love and acceptance were rationed as was the food. The conditions were just right for an acute anxiety neurosis to develop with all my fears jumping up from under the carpet where I had hidden them for years. I managed to keep going and only one or two people knew that I was battling constantly with a fear of illness and of death. Doctors could only tell me there was nothing wrong physically which in no way helped my irrational anxieties.

After eight months, I was pronounced physically fit and ready to go for a full time job. I started applying for anything, anywhere that seemed suitable. Eventually I was called for an interview at the hospital in Orpington. It was a day I shall always remember. Although God was not in my picture at the time, I now believe He was on that roadway leading up to the hospital. It was a most unprepossessing entrance to grim buildings with the wards and physiotherapy department housed in World War One huts. As I walked up the road something (or somebody) within me said 'This is it, this is the place for you'.

Thankfully, those who interviewed me felt the same and my three years there were amongst the happiest of my career. Most of the anxieties began to recede under the carpet not to be brought out again until a later date when I had met someone who knew how to bring about psychological and emotional healing. However, one anxiety remained on the surface. I wanted to be married. In my early childhood I had informed my mother that at the age of 24 I would marry a farmer and have six children, which she would come and look after while I went out riding all day. I do not think she was too enthusiastic about the idea, but I was mad on horses at the time.

Anyway, here I was at the age of thirty still hoping, still expecting marriage would solve all my problems. Each time I moved I thought, 'perhaps this will be the place,' but Orpington had not produced the goods. My hopes rose once again when a friend wrote to me telling me of a job vacancy at the hospital where she worked in Newmarket. It was a good department with an excellent Orthopaedic Surgeon, keen on physiotherapy, and I could live in Cambridge. I was certainly interested.

The interview with the Medical Superintendent was unusual. He was sitting behind his desk at the far end of the room. I knocked, opened the door, tripped on the mat and was catapulted across the room only to be stopped by his desk acting as a crash barrier. I can still see the look on his face! I got the job!

Back to God

I believe that God our heavenly Father turns things and people upside down. I also believe he can take our wrong motives and use them for his purposes. He certainly did this for me soon after I arrived in Cambridge in 1951. I hoped to find a husband; God thought it was more important I should find Him!

As so often before, I once again landed up in a bed-sitting room with a difficult landlady. My first weekend in residence, with my landlady's permission, I had a guest to stay. On the Sunday morning I received a week's notice. We had folded a camp bed at 10 a.m. and her husband said he could not stand the noise! Fortunately, the notice was withdrawn.

In the light of future events it would seem that God had a hand in this, for He needed me to become further acquainted with Alex John, a Christian whom I had met on the day we both arrived in the lodgings. Alex did bring up the subject of God fairly soon but I was embarrassed. I shut her up smartly and wisely she kept silent and waited. In the meantime, feeling lonely and with nothing better to do, I crept out on a couple of Sunday mornings and went to services at an Anglican and a Congregational church, both of which I found boring and largely unintelligible. I am sure Alex was aware of what I was doing because not long after she casually invited me to an evening service.

When I enquired what it was all about, she said it was mainly for students but open to anyone. I think the attraction of students encouraged me to accept and anyway it was something to do on a dull Sunday evening. Little did I think that what happened there would change my life forever.

We sat near the back. I remember nothing of the service or sermon except that the preacher spoke on the famous verse 'Here I am! I stand at the door and knock. If anyone hears my voice and opens the door, I will come in and eat with him and he with me.' (Rev 3v20)

Knowing my background, I cannot believe that this was the first time I heard that I could have a personal relationship with Jesus and only had to open the door and invite him in. But after years in the wilderness what I heard was like offering water to a woman dying of thirst. I knew Jesus was the one whom I needed and wanted.

To my astonishment I found myself walking down the aisle to receive a booklet and give my name and address for a follow-up; not something I would have imagined doing in a million years. For me the experience was totally unexpected but it has been interesting to look back and see some of the seeds which were planted along the way.

During my stay in hospital with my back trouble, I was told that a friend of my mother's had prayed that the surgeon would find the specific cause of the problem. In spite of previous X-rays it was Mr Young's decision to have one more X-ray just before I went to the theatre; this revealed without doubt what was wrong and which operation was needed. During the period when I was in hospital the vicar of the local church dropped in and said they were praying for me. My immediate reaction was very negative but at the same time I was touched that someone should care when I had never entered the church.

In Orpington, I had shared a flat with two girls who knelt down each night in the sitting room and said their prayers. Not to be left out I joined them and recited what I knew - The Lord's Prayer. I am sure these were all seeds which were planted on the good soil of my background to bear fruit years later.

Inviting Jesus into my life was entering into an entirely new phase of my spiritual journey. Stepping out into the unknown in more ways than one. First of all I would like to invite you to read a story, which in a different way illustrates something of my experience. This was written some years after the events described. This is the story of a house – my spiritual house, which I knew I had neglected and which needed re-building.

I asked the very best builder I knew to take on the job. He came and took up residence straight away. Those who knew him told me he would take on any job I asked him to do, cleaning, re-decorating, re-designing, re-furnishing – he was highly skilled and his workmanship was always perfect.

The most amazing thing is that he never sends a bill and he says everything he does comes as a free gift because the account was settled long ago. He has asked me to advertise the fact that he loves re-building people's houses. He doesn't mind how many he does at the same time and he promises to come immediately to anyone who asks for him.

My builder is the Lord Jesus Christ.

So began my life as a committed Christian. I soon knew something had happened: the Sunday service in the Anglican Church, previously boring, suddenly came to life. The Holy Spirit had begun his work. When I approached the Vicar to give me a job, I found myself washing, starching and ironing twelve choirboys' surplices at frequent intervals, not something I would have entertained previously!

I attended the weekly prayer meeting, a strange experience for someone who had never heard the like. What on earth were 'travelling mercies?' To this day I find that phrase difficult and find it easier to pray that I shall be alert to danger, cause no harm to others on the road and be protected by God's holy angels (providing I keep to speed limits!) I think 'travelling mercies' are a condensed version of my prayer. I shall always be grateful for my schooling in extempore prayer though I can still envy other people's fluency.

We came together for these prayer meetings in a bleak dingy hall and knelt to pray on small mats with our elbows on wooden forms. The day came when I thought I must utter a prayer aloud. As I was involved in healing, I thought 'God bless the sick' would be an appropriate start. I practiced it to myself and eventually shot it out. Alex, next to me, said 'I knew you were going to pray because I could feel the bench shaking for a quarter of an hour beforehand!' I still feel like that at times!

I gradually became involved in church life, joined the choir, shared in a fellowship group and continued to wash surplices. Alex was a tower of strength and was very good at discipling me; we studied the Bible together.

Alex and I had not been in our lodgings many weeks when we decided to try and move somewhere with a more congenial atmosphere. Finding new accommodation was not easy in Cambridge so we knocked on doors which produced a few surprises: we called at a home for Franciscan monks and on one occasion were met by a rather surprised lady who, when we enquired if she had rooms informed us that 'Perhaps we did not know but this was a house for unmarried mothers!' We beat a hasty retreat! Eventually we found a very nice household where five of us shared a kitchen but each had her own bed-sitting room.

Our previous unfriendly landlady was not pleased when we gave notice and she ordered us not to bring our suitcases down the only staircase but pointed us to the fire escape. I am afraid we waited until she had gone out and came firmly down the forbidden exit.

We were soon settled in our nice new accommodation but our good fortune was short-lived. One of the residents was engaged to be married to a member of the Cambridge boat crew and would often entertain him and others to breakfast after they had been on their early morning training sessions. One night Joan had a girl friend to stay who had slept on the floor on a mattress. The landlord came in to do an inventory, saw the mattress, saw the boat crew, came to the wrong conclusions and gave all five of us notice. I was actually in Cornwall at the time and was not pleased. A solicitor's letter forced an apology but not a change of heart. Alex and I were on the road again. I was to move twice more, sharing with others until, thankfully, landlords and landladies went out of my life, at least physically!

Becoming a committed Christian changed all my expectations especially the resolutions I made on first arriving in Newmarket when God was not in my reckoning and I could not see into the future. These resolves were: I will not live in Cherryhinton Road, it is too characterless. I will not stay more than two years in the job, in other words if I have not found a husband I will move on. I will never become head of a department; I do not want the responsibility involved.

In fact I bought a flat in Cherryhinton Road, I stayed twenty-three years in my job *without a husband* and became head of the Physiotherapy Department through sad circumstances.

A few months after I arrived the friend who had invited me to Newmarket acquired a more senior post and I was asked to step into her shoes as deputy head. This was fine for a while but it

In the hydrotherapy pool with a patient

became increasingly obvious that my boss was battling with a recurrence of the cancer she had suffered from since before I arrived. She continued to work when she could, but I had to take more and more responsibility for the running of the department. Vi Haytor was a courageous lady; we had many chats during her post-lunch rest and it was a great privilege for me, a babe in the Christian life, to see her, with the vicar's help, come through from fear and unbelief to a real faith in Christ.

There was no healing ministry as such in my church but Kenneth Hooker, the Vicar, put together a beautiful little healing service where Vi received the laying-on of hands. It was my first experience of such a ministry and for me an abiding memory. At this distance in time I cannot remember any details of the service but I can still visualize Vi and myself outside the church, neither of us able to speak. I had the overwhelming sense of being on Holy ground in the presence of Jesus who was enveloping Vi with His peace. We both drove away in our respective cars, still in silence.

Not long after this Vi was taken into hospital. She only had one relative, a cousin, so I visited her regularly and in doing so learned one of those small but very important lessons in life. As I went on holiday I realized that in all my visiting I had not once prayed with Vi. I felt so guilty that I wrote to her and said how sorry I was. I had the most touching letter in reply saying that by my just being with her she knew strength and comfort. I learned through this that though there may have been omissions on my part, words are not always necessary; just being there can be enough.

Vi was not healed of cancer but much more importantly she was healed in mind and spirit; she died in hospital a few weeks later. I had only known her for a short time but I realise that I lost a friend. To my surprise Vi left me £100 to be spent on a holiday. I went with a friend on a Mediterranean cruise, we called at eight ports and it cost us exactly £60 each for the cruise and £40 for the trips. – This was 1954!

Vi also left me the legacy of a very happy well-run physiotherapy department, which was to be my responsibility for the next twenty years, and very much a preparation for the future.

The church I belonged to in Cambridge described itself as 'low evangelical.' I shall always be grateful to the Vicar and others for nurturing me, teaching me and encouraging me in my early days as a Christian.

There was a strong emphasis on missionary work and I suppose it was inevitable that someone should suggest that as a physiotherapist I should go into the mission field to treat those with leprosy. The idea did not ring bells with me and looking back it was obvious that God had planned a different way.

As time went on I found it increasingly difficult to understand and cope with the negative emphasis which kept emerging, albeit from a strong voluble minority, in the church. I must not wear make-up, especially lipstick; I must not go to the cinema or theatre; shock-horror greeted my announcement that I was going to the Footlights, the students' review. It was the final straw when another local Vicar with less rigid views came to speak to our fellowship group and was pronounced by some as unsound. I eventually left and joined his church where I remained throughout my time in Cambridge.

A real breakthrough came when a friend took me down to Lee Abbey, a Christian Holiday and Conference Centre situated in the most beautiful and unspoilt part of the North Devon Coast. For me it was a totally new experience to come to this unique place where under the leadership of an ordained Anglican warden and chaplains at least 50 young Christians gave a year or more of their time to run the house and estate and serve the guests. At the same time they learned what it means to live in community by worshipping, working and living together.

The vision was that guests would come to a beautiful place to come face-to-face with Jesus Christ, some for the first time. Others were refreshed, renewed and taught to go back and bring seeds of new life into their churches. We were there for Easter and for me it was mind-blowing. The teaching, the fellowship, the fun and not least the Easter message were presented in a way which opened my eyes to all that was positive and joyful in being a Christian. I felt I had been blown alive!

For the next ten years my visits to Lee Abbey and their teaching weekends played a very significant part in my Christian growth, not always comfortable but always challenging and I lapped up the teaching, much appreciating the personal talks and prayers with individual members of the community.

It was at Lee Abbey I first experienced the laying on of hands for myself. Never in my wildest dreams did I imagine I would one day become a part of that fellowship and be bringing that ministry to others. I was growing in my spiritual life and I was happily settled in my job, but changes lay ahead.

Loss and Gain

Icould not have found a better hospital than the one in Newmarket in which to settle. The work was varied, interesting and challenging, with patients from all walks of life, not least trainers, jockeys and stable lads, sometimes we were even called upon to treat a race horse!

I was learning how to be a leader and run a department with nine physiotherapists who in the main were in their first job and would move on within two years. It was my aim not only to have an efficient department but also to create an atmosphere which would be for the well-being of both staff and patients. Laughter came high on the list.

This is how it was when in 1960 my parents sold their house in the Wirral and came to live in Bourn, a village outside Cambridge. Michael my brother was married and Jonathan his son was at boarding school in Cambridge. This was a good period when I saw much more of my family. Sadly in 1963, an exceptionally hard winter, my mother slipped on the ice, hit her head and suffered a haemorrhage from which she never recovered.

My mother's death was a major loss for me; in so many ways she had been my lifesaver, particularly in childhood. As an adult my mother supported me in every way, encouraged my independence but was always there if I needed advice or help. We could discuss spiritual things even though we came to the Christian faith from rather different angles. She shared a lot of her pain with me which at times was difficult as I only heard her side of the problem but could see both.

It is a sad fact that I could not give my mother the physical affection she would have liked but I believe she knew I loved her dearly and I am sure I told her that I could not have had a better mother. It sounds a strange thing to say but in terms of my life, the loss of my mother eventually brought immeasurable gain to my spiritual journey. In addition the lessons I learned and the healing I received formed another part of the preparation for that to which God would call me later on in retirement.

Firstly though I need to set the scene for all that I experienced after my mother's death. The week following her accident was one of the most difficult of my life because of the hard decisions I had to make. I had barely recovered from 'flu and was about to go back to my job where I was desperately needed because half the physiotherapy staff were still off sick. At the end of the week, apart from needing a holiday myself, I had promised to escort a friend to Lee Abbey for her convalescence after an operation. What was I to do?

The doctor did not foresee any complications but the treatment for my mother was complete bed rest. My father was there and although willing he was scared of any kind of illness and being a man of his generation his culinary skills were limited.In the end I went back to work and helped where I could each evening. Then, at my mother's insistence, the doctor's agreement and the knowledge that the district nurse and a neighbour would be on hand, I rather reluctantly took my friend down to Devon.

I had only been away one day when there was an SOS for me to return. My mother had been taken into hospital where she was to have an operation. I have always been so thankful that I got back in time for her to know I was there and for us to have a normal conversation before she became confused and two days later died without gaining consciousness after the operation.

So what was it that I experienced after my mother's death that would eventually bring so much gain? Of course I suffered from the natural shock of bereavement but immediately after the funeral I began to suffer a deep sense of guilt mainly centred on the decisions of that last week, the 'if-onlys' swamped my thinking. Repeated confession to God did nothing to bring release from the guilt, most of which I am sure was false. I knew my mother would not have seen things as I did but that did not help; for me it was a real and agonizing experience. I knew guilt false or real should go to the cross but I did not know how to leave it there.

I had two questions, the first immediate: 'What do I do with this guilt?' and later: 'Why did I feel so guilty?' The answer to the first came through a good friend who suggested I went to an Anglican priest whom she recommended as a spiritual adviser and who was used to hearing confessions. This was totally alien to my evangelical thinking but I plucked up courage and in fear and trembling went to confess what I saw as my sins. I can only say what a wonderful relief and release it was to pour out all feelings and fears and guilt to a fellow Christian who took it all quite naturally and then to hear him say 'In the name of Jesus Christ your sins are forgiven.' A burden was lifted, my guilt went to the cross never to be taken back; I felt two stone lighter! I could now echo the words of the hymn 'My chains fell off, my heart was free', – free at least of that particular chain. The second question could only be answered in hindsight: 'Why did I feel so guilty?'

The short answer is that in bereavement I was not thinking straight. The decisions I made during the last week of my mother's life were based entirely on the expectations of a full recovery from the accident. After her death I was looking at those same decisions in the light of what actually happened and naturally found them wanting. The result was false guilt.

It has been a lesson to me that, in grief, thinking can be very twisted. It is easy to get a totally wrong perspective, in consequence false guilt can seem like real guilt. Through finding the answers to my two questions, 'What can I do with my guilt?' and 'Why do I feel guilty?' I can honestly say immeasurable loss has brought immeasurable gain.

After my mother's death my father had the idea that we might live together. I thought about this long and hard but knew it would not work. We had both decided it would be right for me to continue with my job but because our lifestyles and personalities were so different I suggested we would maintain a much better relationship if we lived *near* rather than *with* each other.

Thankfully my father was very understanding. He moved into Cambridge and was soon settled in a flat in the house of a retired lady doctor. She was the best possible landlady who, together with her housekeeper, became real friends to all the family. Doctor Joan and Jean never intruded but kept a loving eye on my father until three weeks before he died in a nursing home.

It so happened that just before my mother's accident I had been told the landlord was selling the house in which I had a flat. For once in my life I was settled in my job and decided it was time I had a home of my own. Single people found it hard to get a mortgage in those days but I managed it and bought a flat only ten minutes away from my father.

I can see myself now, sitting amongst the packing cases – almost weeping with joy and saying 'Thank you Lord. This is my home and no one can turn me out.' I cannot describe what it was like suddenly to be in a place where I could do as I liked without a landlady or landlord directing my life.

I believe we were guided by God to both homes. For the next eight years I kept my freedom, I saw my father blossom and he was very happy in his flat.

We did lots of things together even to going on holiday. I suppose I would describe our relationship as companionable. We were fond of each other.

For me it was the beginning of ten years of stability before retirement which I am sure were within God's perfect plan. He alone knew that in due course he was going to ask me to launch out, not into the wilderness but all over the world. Before that could happen, I needed a period to enjoy a secure job, my own home, a lively church and the leisure activities a city like Cambridge could offer.

One of the activities I enjoyed most was singing with a local choir known as the 'Granta Singers.' I appreciated so many things: the organ and choral scholars who conducted and taught us so much, the friends I made through the choir and all the fun we had, singing in many different venues from evensong in a cold village church to madrigals in punts on the river and carols in the hospital chapel.

I could relate many stories of our adventures. One Remembrance Sunday in a crowded hall a flash bulb exploded loudly as we were quietly singing 'Steal away, steal away, steal away to Jesus.' On madrigal night our oldest member stepped into the river instead of the punt and perhaps my favourite story – in a village church where the seating in the choir stalls was built for small choirboys, not robust altos, we knelt for the Lord's prayer when a loud crack was heard and half the seat fell across our legs. We had six inches on which to perch for the remainder of the service, – wonderful

The Granta Singers on the River Cam at Cambridge

singing and lots of fun!

Altogether life felt very secure and ordered. Choir practice on Monday, House Group on Wednesday, Church on Sunday, time with my father at weekends.

Looking back, I believe that having been such a wanderer I needed that firm physical foundation so that I could look after my father and at the same time God could prepare me for the future by introducing me to a ministry of healing which was very different to my work as a physiotherapist.

The Healing Ministry

In the 1960s the so-called charismatic movement hit Britain and many individuals and churches testified to being totally changed and renewed through a new work of the Holy Spirit, some called it being baptised in the Holy Spirit, something which to me seemed strange and not to be recommended!

Along with everything else I was very involved in the life of my church and although there was no healing ministry as we know it today, I was a member of a prayer group which met weekly to pray for the sick. Looking back, I can see so clearly how God has prompted me to be in the right place at the right time.

I was not a member of the Women's Group in the church but received an invitation to attend a special evening where the speaker was to talk on the subject of 'Healing.'

The speaker's name was Ione Carver who by her own admission was not used to public speaking, but I was riveted by what she shared. She described her own prayer group who had enjoyed meeting together for some years. They studied the Bible, prayed faithfully but felt they were in a rut. New life came to them when the individuals and group were transformed by the power of the Holy Spirit.

This rang bells for me in relation to myself and our prayer group, which Ione could have been describing. I was scared! What would happen if I submitted and asked to be 'Baptised in the Spirit?' Would God immediately eject me to the far corners of the earth? For three weeks following the talk on the Holy Spirit I struggled, talked, prayed, read and then in desperation I asked Peter Vessey, the curate of our church and Uta his wife to pray with me. I am not sure what I expected but nothing startling happened. I did not swing on the chandeliers or erupt in tongues. I just felt warm and comfortable. Later someone at the choir practice asked me if I had a temperature I was so highly coloured!

God did not send me to the farthest corner of the earth but something very important did take place. Almost immediately I knew my heart was open to loving in a way I had not known before. I felt nearer to God and nearer to people, especially my patients. This gift from God was another very important step along the road towards the next milestone.

Peter asked me if I would like to go to a conference on 'healing' at which one of the speakers, an American lady, would be teaching about 'The Healing of Memories.' My 'yes' was one of the most important acts of my life but it was also a great test of my faith. The conference was fully booked with a long waiting list and I was at the bottom.

The day of the conference arrived and there had been no sign of a cancellation. I was longing to telephone and enquire if there was any hope but I felt God was saying, 'No, pack your suitcase and go.' My faith was being exercised as never before but from the beginning I had the strong conviction that I should be there and it would be for my benefit.

It felt very strange walking into the reception area at High Leigh to say, 'I have not got a place, I am on the waiting list, I think I should be here, have you had a cancellation?' – and then to hear the reply 'Yes, as a matter of fact we have, do you have your suitcase with you?' To the applause of those waiting to register I could say 'Yes, as a matter of fact I have my suitcase in the car.' I was in! God knew all the time.

I was in but the weekend was not at all what I expected. On the first night Ann White. the American speaker. got up and said, 'If you are a judgmental person please do not come to my seminars.' - I went hot and cold all over and was in no doubt the Holy Spirit was talking directly to me, 'Yes, Sheila you are judgmental.' The result confused me because I thought my reason for being at the conference was to hear Ann's teaching on the 'Healing of Memories.' At coffee time the following day even as the groups were dividing I was still wavering. Fortunately I ran into one of the conference leaders and cried, 'Help, what shall I do?' His reply was immediate, 'If you are in any doubt do not go to Ann White' s session.' It was a hard decision to go and hear the other speaker, good as he was, and to face the disappointment of my unfulfilled expectations. I fumed throughout the first session. What was God about?

Looking back, I can see how essential it was for me to hear and respond in obedience to those words, 'If you are a judgmental person ..... don't.' The teaching was to come later in God's way and time. It began on the way home.

The drive and the weeks following were to have a very significant effect on my Christian life and all that was to happen in future years of continuing preparation. That weekend Peter Vessey and Uta had been selected to be trained in what was called 'Victorious Ministry' and on the way home Uta shared with me some of the teaching from Ann White's seminars. When she told me that they had been given half an hour in silence with a pencil and paper to write down, under the guidance of the Holy Spirit, any whom they needed to forgive from as far back as they could remember to the present day, my reaction was, 'how unnecessary, not something I need to do.' I do not hold anything against anybody. – I was in for a rude awakening.

The Holy Spirit has a habit of persistent nudging and eventually I capitulated and found myself on my knees with a pencil and minute piece of paper, the expectations were not very high. It was not long before a larger, A4 sheet was necessary!

As I prayed, the Holy Spirit began to show me what lay hidden under the carpet: the people I needed to forgive for words spoken, things unsaid or hurtful actions, all these together with my reactions of anger and resentment still smouldering underneath and still alive. I was amazed at the people and incidents long forgotten that were brought up into my conscious mind.

It was an emotional experience with many tears. Coming to the Cross with the will to forgive those who had hurt me was not easy, remembering the words of Jesus 'Forgive as you have been forgiven' was the only way through. Of course, as I forgave each person individually I also had to receive forgiveness for myself. I look back on this spiritual operation as one of the most significant milestones of my Christian life. So much for my nil expectations!

I felt clean, light and free. It was a major cleansing but only a beginning. A very necessary preliminary to the first prayer counselling I was to receive which would set the scene for years of personal healing and eventually God's call to my own place in the Ministry of Healing. I remember the pink dress I was wearing, I remember the desire to turn and run but above all I remember the amazing grace of God who took two inexperienced counsellors and one scared lady crying 'help' and in one evening began a mighty work of transformation and healing.

What made me suddenly cry, 'help?' There were several reasons. For some years I had prayed for the sick, been involved with the Guild of Health, talked about healing and studied Jesus' healings in the New Testament. But I had applied little of it to myself, certainly not 'The Healing of Memories' which was a new concept. Through the experience of the conference and what followed my eyes were opened to the possibility of inner healing and I could see how much was needed in me. It was God's perfect timing. He was preparing me for the future.

After that first ministry I had the inner conviction that one day I would be involved myself as a prayer counsellor. At the time, training was confined to clergy and pastoral workers but as soon as it was extended more widely, over a period of 3 to 4 years, I attended courses for teaching which included personal prayer counselling as a major part of the training. Through the courses by his Holy Spirit, Jesus came with His healing touch to many areas of my woundedness through family, school and other relationships. One counselling time was of prime importance in terms of my own healing and the future. I can express this best in an allegory by inviting you into the attic of my house.

I often take friends round the house and show them the wonderful things the Lord has done for me, but there is one room into which I never take anyone, usually people do not even notice it because it is tucked away round the corner at the end of a passage. To me it is very special because it is The Lord's Room, He calls it our secret place.

This is where we have all our most intimate conversations. Jesus says He loves to have me with Him there because it is in the times spent alone with Him, that I can really get to know Him, love Him and trust Him more. He says He wants me to share the whole of my life with Him, every joy, every sorrow, every problem and it is only as I sit quietly and listen that He can tell me where He wants me to go and what He wants me to do.

I have never gone into that room without finding Jesus waiting for me. I am ashamed to say He often has to wait for me and I know this hurts Him. Only the other day He reminded me, as He has done many times before, that our secret place is the most important room in the house and if I neglect to come there I am neglecting Him.

There is a calendar hanging over the fireplace and I well remember the text for that day, 'Seek first His kingdom and His righteousness.' Sometimes we sit in the secret place and neither of us speaks. One day we were sitting like this without saying a word, but somehow I could not settle. I knew it was because there was something on my mind which had bothered me for a long time, but which I could not bring myself to talk about. It was rather personal and I knew I would feel embarrassed so kept it to myself and said nothing.

Jesus, as always, sensed my mood. I could feel His eyes upon me and after quite a long time of silence, He picked up the Bible which was lying on the table and passed it over to me, it was open at Psalm 139. I began to read aloud and when I came to the verse, 'Even before a word is on my tongue, lo, O Lord thou knowest it altogether.' I looked up at Jesus. His expression was so loving and He was nodding His head gently as if to say, 'Yes, I do know but I want you to tell me all about it yourself.' I quickly looked down very near to tears, but managed to go on reading until I got to the part which starts, 'For thou didst form my inward parts, thou didst knit me together in my mother's womb . . . Thou knowest me right well,' then I could not hold back the tears any longer. The amazing truth dawned that Jesus really did know everything about me, there was nothing I could keep from Him and I realised that it was only myself from whom I was trying to hide.

This was the key, which unlocked the door. At last some of the things which had been bottled up for years came tumbling out, rather incoherently because words were difficult but I knew that this did not matter.

I said, 'Lord, I seem to be so emotionallly mixed up, afraid to love, afraid to be loved, afraid to show any kind of affection, afraid of rejection. I feel paralysed inside and cannot get out and I have a hard shell outside to stop people getting in. There was a lot more I told Jesus and it was not easy, but as I finished off with a cry of desperation, 'O Lord, I so long to love as you love,' I glanced up at the wall and for the first time noticed the text for the day, it said, 'If the Son makes you free, you will be free indeed.'

I turned to look at Jesus. His whole being told me just how much He loved me and so I knelt at His feet and said, 'Lord, please make me free to love and be loved.' I thought Jesus would lay His hands on my head and I would experience an immediate healing and release, but this did not happen. Instead He took me by the hand and led me out of the secret place to the foot of the ladder which goes up into the attic. He said, 'I want you to go up there and . . .' I did not allow Him to explain further, but protested loudly saying, 'But Lord, I've asked you to make me free not send me on wild goose chases up ladders into attics, whatever good will that do?' Jesus gently silenced my protests and said, 'You did not let me finish. I think you have forgotten that you have stored a good many unwanted goods in the attic and these need clearing away before you can be free.' I knew Jesus was right, I had pushed a pile of stuff up into the attic in the hope that out of sight would be out of mind. I also knew it would have to be faced one day and now the day had come.

The Lord said, 'You go up first and I will follow shortly.' As I went up the ladder, my heart grew heavier and heavier and I dreaded what would meet me in the attic. It was dark as I climbed through the trap door, only a faint gleam of light came from the skylight. To my surprise the room appeared to be empty, I certainly did not fall over any of the expected boxes. As my eyes grew accustomed to the gloom, I noticed there was something in the middle of the room, which looked like a wooden hut. It was very mysterious, but I felt drawn to go inside. It was light enough for me to see that I was in a kind of naturalist's hide, with a closed shutter on each wall and benches to sit on. There was even a pair of binoculars hanging up on a peg. It was rather eerie and I felt strangely cold and alone. I did not quite know what to do, so I sat on one of the benches. No sooner had I done so than one of the shutters fell down with a clatter and I nearly jumped out of my skin. I looked out and thought I must be seeing things, because I could just make out what looked like the shapes of people in the far distance. I remembered the binoculars and used these to get them into focus. I could see a man and a woman sitting sideways to me, some way apart with their backs to each other. Facing me and in between them was a small child, looking utterly bewildered and lost. I could not understand what it was all about. Suddenly the child got up and went running to the woman who was obviously her mother, who picked her up and hugged her and then she went running to her father, who had a game with her and so she went on to and fro and to and fro. I could see the child was longing for them all to come together so that she did not have to keep running from one to the other, but the Father and Mother stayed apart and neither looked at or spoke to each other. Eventually the child gave up and came back to her chair. She looked as though she was about to cry, but instead she picked up a little dog who was licking her hand and she seemed to find comfort in burying her head in his coat. It was then I recognised her and there crept over me the most awful sensation of being torn apart inside and then frozen.

That picture faded and another shutter fell down with a resounding clatter. Once again I saw people. I thought I recognised the same child a few years older. This time, she was standing in what appeared to be a school playground. She looked lonely and frightened. Nearby a group of children were playing together and as she went up to try and join them, they all spun round and shrieked, 'We are not going to speak to you for a whole week,' and then ran off laughing to the other end of the playground. Once again I knew who it was; the cold inside me grew almost unbearable and I felt sore and bruised from head to foot. I wanted to cry but could not.

The last shutter fell down with the biggest crash of all. It was not a child I saw this time, but a woman. I could not see her face properly, but I got the impression that she had a kind of longing look. There were a few men standing around and I watched her go up to one, then another and another, the pattern was the same every time. She went up and held out her arms as if to say, 'Please love me,' and each one just shook his head, turned and walked away until she was left alone. At the moment of her aloneness, I was aware not only of being frozen inside and bruised, but also felt a mixture of shame, hurt and rejection which nearly overwhelmed me and I heard myself crying out, 'Lord Jesus, I cannot bear any more.' As soon as I called, He was there and His arms went round me and held me tight until I had calmed down. We were still in the hut and I was longing to get out of it and go downstairs again. I told Jesus this, but He said, 'There is something else you must do before you go. I want you to look out and be a part of those scenes again.' For the second time that day I protested loudly and said, 'Lord, I cannot possibly go through all that again, it's not fair to ask it of me.' Jesus replied very lovingly, 'Do not be afraid, I shall be near you and this time there will be healing, not fear.' And so I opened the first shutter again and looked out. It was all exactly the same until the child came back to her chair and then I saw Jesus was there, He picked her up in His arms and her whole face lit up as she hugged Him; she looked as though she knew she was completely safe and secure. Jesus' presence had an effect too on the mother and father and they turned, looked at each other and came towards Him and the child. I knew I did not need to look any more. It was so wonderful and I felt a little warmth creep inside me as though the ice had begun to melt.

The second scene was equally wonderful. Again it was just the same until the children ran off and then instead of the child left alone, bewildered and hurt, I saw Jesus come up, take her by the hand and talk to her and play with her. She was laughing and happy and seemed to know that she had a real friend who would never let her down or run from her. As the scene faded I realised some of the bruising and soreness had gone.

Finally, I watched again the woman being rejected by one man after the other, but at the very end I saw her going to meet someone who had His arms outstretched towards her. I knew it was Jesus and as He reached out and took both her hands, I heard Him say to her, 'I have loved you with an everlasting love.' She looked up into His face with such joy and at the same time, I heard Jesus saying this to me and I too experienced a joy and awareness that here was a love so great and so sure that in Him I need never again fear rejection. As the shutter closed for the last time, my tears began to flow and this time I made no attempt to stop them, it was as if all the bottled up emotions of the years were being released. Jesus did not try and stop me, He just held me tight and I knew this was all part of the healing.

After a time when I was able to look up, I was surprised to find we were no longer in the hut, in fact it had disappeared and the attic looked like any normal empty room. There seemed to be no reason to stay any longer and I wanted to get out as soon as possible. When I reached the door I took one last look back and there right in the middle of the room where the hut had been, I could see a hill and on top, three crosses. The middle one stood out, Jesus was hanging on that cross. I heard myself quietly singing, 'See from His head, His hands, His feet, sorrow and love flow mingled down; did e'er such love and sorrow meet or thorns compose so rich a crown.' The room became empty again and I went down into the passage. Jesus closed the trap door, sealed it and then removed the ladder. As we walked downstairs, He gave me such a lovely smile and said, 'The attic now belongs to me, I am the Lord.'

It was wonderful to get back to our secret place, all I wanted to do was to sit quietly. I was content just to be near Jesus, to love and to worship Him. After some while, I got up from my chair and as I did so something dropped off me and crashed to the floor, leaving me with a curious feeling of lightness and freedom. Jesus stooped to pick it up, but before it melted away in His hands, I just had time to recognise it as the shell I had worn around me for so many years. I knelt at Jesus' feet and He put His hands on my head. As He did so I could feel His love flowing freely into every part of me and at the same time it seemed to flow out from me. I knew in my heart that my prayer for love was answered and that this flowing in and out would never cease as long as I kept close to the Lord.

Jesus lifted me to my feet and turned me round to face the text on the wall, which said, 'Now the Lord is the spirit and where the spirit of the Lord is, there is freedom. And we all with unveiled face, beholding the glory of the Lord, are being changed into His likeness from one degree of glory to another; for this comes from the Lord who is the Spirit.'

During those training years, I was continually experiencing the truth of the words of scripture 'He who began a good work in you will carry it on to completion until the day of Christ Jesus.' (Phil. 1 v 6).

After completing three training schools, the invitation came for me to attend one or two courses each year as a member of the team involved with those who were coming forward for counselling and training. So many people, like myself, were testifying to changed lives in all that God was revealing and healing through this prayer counselling ministry that there was an increasing demand from clergy and laity alike, for places on the schools.

The ministry was now established in England and the name was changed from 'Victorious Ministry' to 'Wholeness Through Christ.'

My call had come and I was terrified! Many times in the early years of involvement with the WTC ministry I was tempted to give up and give in to the constant struggles, the feelings of inadequacy and the fatal, unhelpful comparisons with others who seemed so much more confident and in tune with God than I was. The problem was not helped by my fear of men, especially authority figures and clergy. Thankfully, God continued in me His good work of healing in this area and at the same time friends encouraged me to stick with it, truly believing (as I did) that I was called to the ministry.

How grateful I am that I ran the race because the Wholeness Through Christ teaching and counselling was to be the basis of much of the work I was to do at Lee Abbey in my retirement years.

Looking back, I can see many areas of learning needed to take me forward into retirement: learning the skills of leadership in charge of a physiotherapy department; the cut and thrust of being a member of a church house group; learning the skills of communication and bible study with a small number of people; training in evangelism, learning to share my faith – all essential ingredients for the activities of the future.

All the time when I was learning about the ministry for the healing of memories and emotions and benefiting from it, I was continuing with my normal job in the hospital concerned with the physical healing of patients. In addition, as my father grew more frail I was spending more time with him. I shall always be grateful that the circumstances of my father's death were so very different to that of my mother's.

As I have said before, my father was a private man and even though in his last years we spent more time together he was seldom able to show or share his feelings and we never talked about anything emotional, or spiritual, which concerned me. He was interested in church architecture and in the latter part of his life went to church regularly but I had no idea what he really believed or felt about dying. I knew it was important for my sake as well as his but did not know how best to bring up the subject. My prayer for help was answered in an unusual way a few days before he died.

My father had an old college friend, Malcolm, a deeply committed Christian, who was as concerned as I was that he had never been able to discuss spiritual things with my father. He had always met with a brick wall. During my father's time in the nursing home when he was very weak I read him a letter from Malcolm in which he said, 'Dying for a Christian is like passing from school to college.' This was my cue to ask, 'Do you believe that?' Miraculously his 'Yes' then opened the door for me to pray with him each night. This was not quite the end. At 7.30 a.m. one Sunday morning a verse from the Bible seemed to leap out of the page 'I tell you the truth, a time is coming and has now come when the dead will hear the voice of the Son of God and those who hear will live' (John 5:25). At 8.00 am the telephone rang summoning me to the nursing home where late in the evening my father died. I believe he heard the voice of the Son of God. He died in 1971 and three years later I would reach a very significant milestone on my journey but the approach road was quite rough and stony.

Sheila's father William Geoffrey Stevens

Facing Retirement

I was looking towards retirement. Fifty-five was a legitimate age for a physiotherapist to retire and receive a pension though the hospital would have been happy for me to continue for another five years.

I think I chose to for two reasons. Firstly, I had been in the job for thirty-five years and wanted to be young enough and free to do other things, and secondly as a Christian, although there had been no writing on the wall or specific scriptural confirmation, I had a long-held conviction that this was the right decision.

So the choice had been made, my resignation accepted and a successor appointed; there was no turning back. My career as a physiotherapist was coming to an end and I panicked:'What am I going to do? Will I have enough money to live on? How can I manage without people? Am I really doing God's will?' I needed to go upstairs in my 'house' to find some of the answers.

All these years Jesus has been the perfect landlord and friend, talking, listening, guiding, forgiving and above all loving. He has never failed me and never forsaken me. One way and another life until last year seemed to be going pretty smoothly. I had a satisfying enjoyable job, enough money, lots of friends, a nice flat and a good church. In fact all the things that the average person considers necessary for a happy and contented life.

Then, suddenly one day I realised that the whole pattern of my contented living was going to change and with that realisation all the walls of security came crashing down leaving me exposed and frightened.

I had often sat with Jesus in the sitting room of the house asking Him what He wanted me to do about retiring from my job. He knew I did not need to go but all along I had the feeling He had other plans in mind for me.I tried hard to get them out of Him, it would have made the decision so much easier, but He said, 'No, not yet, you keep saying you trust me, now I want you to prove that trust. Go away, and think what I promised you in my word the other day. I thought and remembered – 'The Lord will fulfil His purpose for me' (Psalm 138:8) – I had to say to Jesus, 'Your love Lord goes on for ever (Psalm 138) forgive me and I do trust you!'

That trust did not last very long; as soon as the decision to retire was made, my house went into chaos. The fact that I had decided to go abroad for four months made it even more chaotic. Jesus was about of course; He looked very sad and I knew it was because of me, but I seldom stayed long enough with Him to hear what He had to say. I was off and up the stairs to count my money or to chew over the foolishness of leaving a nice secure job, or to wonder if I was going to be ill in the Australian bush.

After a time I would rush downstairs and find Jesus and shout at Him, 'For goodness sake help me, I do not know what to do, I've made a wrong decision, I am not going to have enough to live on. Am I really doing your will?' And on and on. Once or twice I did stay with Jesus just long enough to hear His reply: His were always words of assurance. Once I can remember Him saying, 'Do not be afraid I am with you wherever you go.' I was immensely comforted for two or three days but then went tearing round the house again. One day my legs were aching so much from running up and down stairs I actually sat down quietly in the sitting room. For once I was neither chewing over my own problems nor shrieking for help. I suddenly became aware of Jesus sitting next to me with His love just enfolding me. This time I had no difficulty in hearing what He was saying. He was reading Psalm 121 and as He neared the end He put His arms round me and said, 'You are doing my will, there is nothing to fear, I am going with you to the other side of the world. I will bring you back safely and nothing can separate you from my love.' As He finished speaking a peace such as I have seldom known stole right through me and I knew it could be none other than the peace which passes all understanding (Phil.4:7)

After a long time of quiet Jesus said, 'Now I want you to take me upstairs and show me those rooms where you have spent so much time in the last few weeks. My peace was momentarily shattered when I realised what this meant. I had sometimes let Jesus come to the door of the rooms and look quickly round, but I had never invited Him right in because as I often told Him, 'I must have some privacy' and I was sure He would respect this. He always did.

Now I knew the time had come when my privacy had to go. I was a bit scared of what it would mean and rather ashamed at the thought of what Jesus would see. I had no time to go and re-arrange anything. We walked slowly up the stairs and when we got to the first door there was a notice on it I had never seen before: it said 'My Security is in My money.' We could hardly get inside the door for the waste paper littering the floor. The pieces of paper on which I had done frantic sums trying to see if I was going to be able to make ends meet. In the middle of the room was a table on which was a large account book. I did not really want Jesus to look at this because it held all my private accounts showing how I had spent my money and I knew it was not always wisely. Jesus went straight to the table and called me over. I went hesitantly shuffling through the mounds of paper. To my amazement when I looked at the book there was not a single figure on the paper but instead illuminated in the most beautiful lettering the words, 'My God will supply all your needs according to His riches in the Glory of Christ Jesus.' I just stared at the words and then felt Jesus gently leading me away to the next room where it said on the door, 'My Security is in my job and in my status.' Once again we could hardly get inside the door, but this time we were falling over beds and wheelchairs, people in plaster and on crutches. As soon as they saw me they started shouting – 'you are too young to retire – we need you to treat us – please do not leave us in the lurch.' When they saw Jesus they suddenly quietened down as if reassured by His presence. He led me over to a desk I used for all the administrative work on which there was always the book for entering the patients' statistics. I did not want Jesus to see this because He would know from the numbers what a lot of extra work I was leaving them to do. Once more I went hesitantly and was astonished to see my tatty old book transformed and instead of columns of figures the words, 'Trust in the Lord with all your heart and lean not to your own understanding. Acknowledge Him in all your ways and He will direct your paths.' He handed me what looked like a treatment card – Your status – a Child of God, a King's daughter, an Heir of the Kingdom.

I let the words sink in as I went towards the final room and again I saw words on the door, 'My security is in the familiar.' There appeared to be nothing in the room apart from two empty chairs facing what looked like a television screen. Jesus invited me to sit down and as I did so the screen lit up and I began to see a moving presentation of all that had been familiar to me for many years – the hospital where I had worked, the choir in which I had sung, my flat which was such a lovely home after years of living in bed-sits. Amidst the scenes I saw all the people with whom I'd shared my life over the years. I didn't want to let anything go, it was all so familiar and safe. As scenes continued to flash before my eyes, I was aware of a voice beside me which somehow penetrated my whole being – 'Sheila, do you love me more than these?' It seemed like hours before I could speak. It was one of the hardest and most direct questions Jesus had ever asked me. As I turned to look at Him, He was bathed in the most beautiful light and when I looked into His eyes and saw in them such an amazing love for me that the only answer I could give was, 'Yes, Lord, I love you more than these.'

I had hardly said, 'Yes, Lord,' when Jesus held out His hand to me. As I put mine in His and felt a strength and a warmth quite beyond human touch, a great joy surged through me and I was glad I had let Him into those rooms. The television screen which had gone dark suddenly lit up and across it was written 'God alone is my rock and my salvation, He is my fortress, I shall never be shaken. The Lord will watch over my coming and going both now and for ever more.'

We walked back along the corridor and I saw the notices on the doors, were changed: they were all the same – 'My Security is in the Lord Jesus Christ, My Lord and My God.'

Two weeks before I left the hospital I was given a party at a local hotel when at least thirty physiotherapists who had worked with me over the years came back for the occasion. It was a farewell but at the same time a wonderful reunion: an evening to remember.

The really hard parting came on 7th June 1974, my fifty fifth birthday when I walked out of the Physiotherapy Department at Newmarket General Hospital for the last time. I had worked very happily there for twenty-three years and I could not face saying goodbye. I told the staff I wanted to walk out as though it was an ordinary Friday evening; this was a mistake that would catch up with me years later. My life as a physiotherapist had lasted thirty-five years. There had been good times and bad times with a mixture of experiences but it was such a privilege to be part of a 'healing ministry.' I had no regrets for my chosen career; it was so people-orientated therefore always challenging, full of interest and a lot of fun.

Looking back I can see the leadership responsibilities I held for twenty years as head of a department, together with involvement with people of all ages and walks of life, were a wonderful preparation for what lay ahead, the unknown future.

My long-term expectations for retirement were minimal. In the short term I had planned a two-week holiday in Israel and a four-month visit to Australia and New Zealand to see friends.

My only seed thought for the future was the possibility of a year at the local Bible College; I had a desire to learn more of the Bible. This seed was sown by three young people a year or so before I retired. I knew Paul Booth and John Cooper as members of our church youth group and through them I met Janet Wilton (now

Fickling). As far as I remember when I came on the scene Paul and Janet had finished their course at Romsey House and John was still there, like me somewhat concerned for the future.

Two things happened, one which nearly cost me my reputation and the second which gave me a very special friendship with Janet which over the years has grown to include Roger, Janet's husband and their daughter Suzie. To go back to my reputation, John and I, both in the same boat regarding our future, decided we would support each other and pray together once a week. The most convenient time would be 7.00 am before I had to leave for work. We did this regularly for some weeks.

I lived in a second floor flat and had a neighbour on the ground floor who spent a lot of his time at the window or outside the front door. One day he could not resist asking me if I knew who owned the mini which was parked outside the flats every Wednesday morning? I told him the truth and then learned that several of the residents in my block hung out of their windows each week hoping to catch a glimpse of my toy boy! Fortunately my reputation survived but it made me realise how easy it could be to lose it! Apart from John and I meeting together the four of us would link up for a meal, pray for each other, laugh a lot and share our dreams.

How we got round to it I do not know but we decided we would like to live together as a household community, run it as a home where people could come for rest and refreshment, maybe for a retreat, even a small conference. None of us had any money and certainly no experience but Paul went off to an estate agent to collect the keys for a very large house in a spacious garden outside Cambridge. We went round solemnly discussing the suitability of the place for our dream. Fortunately we came to our senses, realized it was a nightmare, had a good laugh and admitted that God was not that stupid even if we were.

Had I not spent all that time with my three friends things might have been different but to me looking back they were God-sent, for the seed bore fruit and with their encouragement I went for an interview with the principal of the college who suggested we both pray about it during the time I was in Australia and make a decision on my return.

Apart from this I imagined I would stay in Cambridge where I lived and enjoy the relief of not having to drive twenty-six miles a day in all weathers, with no more set hours, set holidays or weekends on call. Without responsibilities, life would be one long holiday. I could not have been more wrong!

Had I known beforehand what was going to happen I am sure I would have said, 'No thank you, please leave me alone in my nice safe, familiar, comfortable surroundings. I will be involved in my church, entertain my friends and enjoy singing in the choir. I am retired now. Fortunately God knew me and kept his revelations to himself until I was ready, ready to face each stage of the journey when there would be so many changes, so many new discoveries and so many surprises.

Looking back, I can also see that God spent my whole lifetime preparing the ground for a very exciting future. First of all it was New Zealand and Australia.

CHAPTER 9

New Zealand and Australia

For years I had dreamed of visiting a school friend in Australia. Nancy Dickson lived with her husband Dickie in the beautiful city of Perth. Every Christmas she had written to say, 'When are you coming?' At last my dream could become a reality; I was retired and I could go ahead. God was in my dream.

I have always loved boats and was keen to go to Australia by sea. I was nervous at travelling this way by myself and could not see the answer to either sharing a cabin with three strangers or alternatively a single cabin at vast expense. The problem was solved when Sara Jones, (now Wright), an ex-member of my physiotherapy staff whom I liked very much telephoned, out of the blue, to ask if I would mind if she travelled to Australia with me!

This was a God-given gift. We originally planned to travel out together and then part company but our respective friends generously invited us both to stay so my dream was enlarged to include New Zealand as well as unexpected journeyings in Australia. After three months, we eventually arrived in Perth for our six-week stay.

The voyage to New Zealand took 5½ weeks. Apart from the excitement of going ashore at all the ports of call, life on the ship produced plenty of drama. Half way between Southampton and Bermuda all passengers were summoned to the main deck to be informed by the Captain there was a bomb scare, so our voyage began by our sitting in life jackets beside the lifeboats until it was known some hours later that the scare was a hoax. After two fires and a hurricane warning, we decided there must be too many Christians on board! I felt quite at peace remembering that earlier promise 'The Lord will watch over your coming and going . . .'

Before I left England I prayed that if there were other Christians on board I would meet them. It could hardly have been a coincidence that out of 1,000 passengers five Christians ended up at our table: Sara and myself, together with an ex-missionary and a young Australian couple.

We met to pray and decided to start meeting for a Bible Study on the days we were at sea. The Purser was not willing to advertise it on the daily newssheet distributed to every cabin, because this would set a precedent for any other group to advertise. A minute card on the notice board attracted two people, a good beginning increasing our number to seven, but God was on our side and the Purser did not have a leg to stand on when a Rotary Club meeting was mentioned in the morning news!

Fortunately we had a retired Bishop on board whose status enabled him to intervene for us with the Captain, for as our numbers grew we had to keep asking for a larger venue, which was not popular with the Purser! Before we reached New Zealand an interdenominational group of around thirty people were meeting together. – Too many Christians?!

At our first Bible Study after leaving San Francisco I found myself sitting next to two strangers who had obviously just come on board. I recognised one of them as Agnes Sanford, the writer of many books on Christian Healing. She was then over 80 and was visiting Australia and New Zealand to give lectures. She was travelling with Enid, a companion, primarily there to guard her privacy.

Fortunately, neither of them saw Sara and myself as invaders. We spent a great deal of time with them both and so enjoyed Agnes' delightful sense of fun and gift for story telling. In all seriousness though she told us she was aware of angels surrounding the ship. With the various potentially dangerous happenings on the ship I am sure she was right. I found it a great privilege to talk and pray with this deeply spiritual lady and I came away with some lovely memories and two gems which have not faded with time.

The first related to the possibility of my going to Bible College after returning to England. It was an Agnes Sanford prayer asking that if Bible College was in God's plan for me the thought would be insistent and grow warmer but if it was not within God's will the thought would grow cold and die. In spite of the fact that I was preoccupied with seeing new sights, learning from new experiences and meeting new people, I do not think a day went past, in the months away, when at some point my mind would not alight on Romsey House and the thought came with increasing warmth. Time and time again I have prayed a similar prayer for others seeking God' s way.

The second gem came as a surprise and challenged my thinking. We persuaded Agnes Sanford to give us a talk at our last Bible Study before docking in Auckland. I am sure the subject was prayer and during question time at the end a man asked her angrily why he had been praying for a lady with arthritis for fifteen years and she had not been healed? The reply was short 'It was probably not your responsibility to be praying for her.' The lesson which has stayed with me over the years is that 'A need does not necessarily constitute a call.'

Sara and I were very sad when the voyage came to an end. We had so enjoyed life on board the Oronsay, the leisurely days at sea, the varied ports of call from Bermuda to Fiji and a wonderful day going through the Panama Canal: just what was needed for the first weeks of retirement.

We spent three weeks in New Zealand travelling on local buses, visiting friends and seeing a great variety of scenery in that beautiful country.

Much as I loved New Zealand, I found Australia more exciting: it was so unlike anything I had seen before. My chief memories would be of the vast areas of bush in the Blue Mountains, the opera house and harbour in Sydney, the little penguins on Philip Island near Melbourne and the glorious wild flowers on the west coast outside Perth.

Everything was so different even to kangaroos hopping about in the wild and kookaburras with their extraordinary laugh. We had travelled across the world, visited many friends, seen wonderful sights: it had been a memorable holiday but after four months we were ready to fly home. For me, would it be Romsey House?

The **Oronsay,** *ready to cast off*

Romsey House

The never-to-be-forgotten voyage to New Zealand and Australia was over, retirement was about to begin in earnest. Mrs Jock Habermann, the principal of Romsey House Theological College said, 'Yes.' I said, 'Yes' and so from being head of the physiotherapy department at Newmarket Hospital I became a nervous, very mature student attending the College on a daily basis. My aim was to learn more of the Bible and I was privileged to attend lectures but be excused from writing essays, taking exams, going out on pastoral projects.

In so many ways it could not have been better as a transition into retirement. I had a routine, was being mentally stimulated and was in a community alongside young people just as I had been in all the years of working in hospital. But there was a marked difference: the sudden realisation that I had lost my role and status and changed from being a somebody in authority to a nobody under authority. It hit me hard and all I could think and say was 'Who am I?'

After a year of study I still had not solved the problem of my identity but I was offered two options for the future. Either to stay at the college and do a lay reader's course, or to join the staff of Holy Trinity, the city centre church which I attended in Cambridge.

I have never enjoyed or found studying easy and I could not feel any particular call towards being a lay reader, so I decided the second option was the right one. As it happened I did stay on at Romsey House for another eighteen months in a rather different capacity: laying tables, stirring the puddings and searching for dust in the students' rooms, – not requiring much search in some of them! Certainly it was a contrast to the life of a physiotherapist but I enjoyed it. Alongside the search for dust, I was still searching for an identity.

I was going to the weekly staff meetings but they only aggravated the problem as I had no defined role and no particular title. I struggled with being introduced to a new staff member as 'just Sheila' as I did not quite know who 'Sheila' was! My laugh was somewhat hollow when it was suggested my title should be 'Jesus' little ray of sunshine!'

Those meetings which so highlighted my identity crisis were the best thing that could have happened to me. God used them to bring home the truth of who I was and who I am. In facing the loss of the role and status on which I was so reliant for my security I began to face the much more important reality that my status was and always will be as a Child of God and an heir of the Kingdom. My role is to follow Jesus wherever He leads. Now I am quite content to be 'just Sheila'; I like it. I am not so sure about a 'little ray of sunshine!'

Going back to the first year at Romsey House and my identity crisis there was one other problem. The College year was divided into terms and I was going to be faced with a whole summer with nothing to do and nowhere to go.

During my thirty-five years as a physiotherapist I had been confined to one month's holiday a year. Sabbaticals were unheard of for hospital workers and here was I with a yawning gap of three months. Part of the gap was filled as a team leader at a Christian Holiday Camp for girls. It turned out to be one of the longest weeks of my life. I love children in ones and twos but as a gaggle I only succeed in boring them while I am unable to maintain discipline. As a physiotherapist a class for children with flat feet had been my biggest nightmare. It became very clear to me that my future ministry would most likely be with adults. I think the camp leader agreed!

Only to be occupied for one week during the summer was not what I wanted. I was single with no family ties or responsibilities. I lived in a flat without a garden so I could shut the door and walk out with the freedom to go anywhere and do anything; so what was I to do? The most positive thing to do first of all was to pray what seemed a good prayer for seeking God's guidance for the unknown future. 'Here I am Lord, do with me what you will, send me where you will; your will be done.' This is a prayer I have used constantly during my years of retirement; dangerous, yes, but one I have never regretted, for doors have been opened beyond my wildest dreams.

Having prayed I started knocking. One day I saw an advertisement requesting summer workers at a Christian holiday centre in Grange-over-Sands. I was not too distressed when my application was turned down because they were afraid that living accommodation in a shared caravan would not be suitable for a lady of my advanced years. I agreed, preferring comfort and solitude. In the light of what was to come, this was laughable!

One day a visiting preacher came to our church from the Intercontinental Church Society. He was obviously speaking primarily to students inviting them to join a small team going out to a Spanish resort to take part in an evangelistic enterprise which would involve talking to British holidaymakers in the tourist hotels. My mind focused on a trip to Spain staying in a nice comfortable hotel. This would suit me well during the summer, I thought. I hardly heard the work 'evangelism.' I have the feeling that God blocked my ears because he wanted a response! So I spoke to the preacher who saw no reason why an older person should not be involved as there were many older tourists going abroad on package holidays. He promised to go back to the Society and consult his colleagues.

I heard nothing for some weeks and one morning prayed that if this venture was God's will I would be contacted. Half an hour later the phone rang and a voice said 'Yes please, we would like you to join a team. You will be camping and visiting hotels in Sitges. I could hardly believe my ears – me, camping; not even a caravan! Worse was to come: camping involved a trailer tent in which four of us would sleep top to tail. My mind whirled round possible excuses to opt out but I knew I was committed and must go through with the venture. The next step did not encourage me.

David and Shirley Steele, who headed up the whole project for InterCon, called us together for a weekend in London. This was for information, training and to meet the seven other members of the team who were all strangers to me and to one another. The weekend did little to allay my fears. In years to come David and Shirley have often laughed with me about my apparant state of permanent shock throughout our two days together. Not surprisingly, I was the oldest member of the team by some years and even though it was only for two weeks, the whole operation grew bigger and more scary in my mind.

My worst fear came when we were sent out in twos into Earl's Court to stop people and ask them if they would spare a few minutes to answer a few questions about Christianity. We had an official questionnaire to help them. To my surprise some put down their shopping baskets and obliged. One girl was even converted on her own doorstep.

This, together with the Bible teaching, was the preparation for going out into the hotels in Spain to talk to holidaymakers who would be sitting around without television and with time on their hands. This was the beginning of

God's open door to five summers of 'Purpose Holidays' taking the Gospel to various resorts in Spain.

It gave me some experience of the most awesome, scary, humorous events and encounters in faith building to treasure for ever as one of God's amazing gifts in retirement. Also, it proved God knew me better than I knew myself. I loved camping.

On the training weekend I had met my leader, Diana Eady (now Robbins). She had previously asked me on the telephone if I would travel out with her in her mini taking a trailer with all the camping equipment. The idea was for me to share the driving. The day before we set off I discovered my driving licence was out of date!

We were both wary of each other, Diana wondering what she had taken on with this elderly lady in a state of shock who did not like camping and for my part how I was going to cope with the whole affair, not least, cooped up in a mini for four days with a strange companion who was expecting me to share the driving.

As it turned out at my confession, Diana said 'Don't worry I like driving' which warmed me to her immediately and my feelings were further endorsed when she produced delicious ham sandwiches to eat on the ferry. Diana warmed to me when I did what I was told when erecting the trailer tent and didn't grumble at sleeping in it!

We had an interesting journey especially when the mini objected to climbing the Pyrenees and had to be taken off the boil at regular intervals for a rest and a thermos of cold water! By the time we got to Sitges, after four days travelling, Diana had done all the driving, I had cooked all the meals, we knew each other's life history and had become the best of friends.

CHAPTER 11

Evangelism in Spain

Before we went out to Spain David Steele and Shirley visited all the hotel managers so that we had permission to go into the hotels and talk to their visitors. It was estimated that at least 80% of those approached with the questionnaire were willing to answer and sometimes conversations would continue for two or three hours.

We encountered different responses: ignorance, opposition and genuine interest. Much of what we were doing was seed sowing but we certainly saw the Holy Spirit at work. I remember one unbelieving, sceptical man ending up our hour-long conversation by saying 'You have thrown a lot of pebbles in the pond and the ripples will go on.'. . .

I remember one of many drunken yobos who, after sobering up, responded to the Gospel and committed his life to Jesus Christ. He shared in our daily Bible studies and then came with us to witness in the hotels. We constantly experienced the word of God as living and active. It was a privilege to be with a lady who read some verses of scripture aloud, very haltingly, and then to see the light dawn on her face as the truth was revealed.

Going up to strangers risking rebuff was never easy but the encouragements always outweighed the fears. I could tell more stories of encounters over the years but I want to share three incidents which will always be uppermost in my memory because through them we have experienced God at work in such very different ways.

One evening, on the first of my Purpose Holidays, we decided to visit holidaymakers on the campsite. For some reason we were an odd number and I volunteered to go on my own. I went down to the lowest level, spotted a British car and an open tent. Looking inside I could only see men lying around on the floor. My courage failed and I wandered up and down praying, at the same time saying, 'no way; I can't!' I decided the sensible decision was to return to our tents to see if one of the men was free to go with me. Walking up the steps, I distinctly heard a voice which said, 'Go back.' There was no person within sight and I knew somehow that it must be the voice of God. I had never experienced anything like it before, nor have I had any such experience since.

Fortunately I retraced my steps and as I did so one of the men came out to hang his socks on the line. I was able to approach him and he invited me into the tent where there were two other men and a girl. I still can hardly believe what followed. I sat on the ground for two hours being opposed by a lapsed and very bitter Roman Catholic, a member of the Orange Order and an angry young atheist. I felt totally unruffled and was very aware that I was being guided by the Holy Spirit. The only remark I remember was when the angry young man said, 'If that's the sort of God you've got I don't want him.'

All the time we were talking, I was aware that the infrequent remarks made by the girl showed there was some interest; she was the wife of the atheist. To keep contact with her I decided to invite them all for coffee at our camp site the following evening. There was no immediate response, but to our surprise the next night all four trooped in.

If ever I was asked to name one particular occasion when the Holy Spirit was tangible, it would be on that night. We experienced our team coming together as the Body of Christ inter-acting in an amazing way as our guests shared their pain, their questions and their doubts. There was silent prayer, quiet music, listening, talking and reading the scriptures, with the Holy Spirit drawing all the threads together.

I continued to sense the interest of Laura (not her real name) and managed to give her the name of her local church together with my address. The next day I reluctantly returned home to go to the holiday camp!

The story did not finish on the camp site; in fact it had only just begun. Three months later I had a letter from Laura telling me that she had committed her life to Christ and Harry (not his real name) her husband was going to church with her. Three months later, another letter; Harry had committed his life to Christ and they were both going out on missions. A few months later Harry was going into training for the ordained Ministry!

I do not think I shall ever forget that camp site and the privilege it was for us as a team to be used for God's purposes and see Him at work in such a wonderful way, – also to see the results. I shall always be thankful that I turned and went back. Most of the time we did not see what followed after one conversation. This was the case in my second story.

Normally, we went out in twos. On one particular evening John and I were together and it was my turn to initiate a conversation. We approached a retired couple who were willing to answer the questionnaire. The wife was a silent partner but the man on hearing the first question, 'In your opinion what is a Christian?' spent a quarter of an hour airing all his pet theories and objections to Christianity. When I finally managed to get a word in and ask him the last question which was 'if you could know Jesus Christ personally, would you like to?' to my astonishment he said, 'Yes.' When I appeared intrigued he said, 'Yes, I know you know Jesus.' I had to ask him how he knew. His reply has stayed with me. He said 'I know you know Jesus because you have listened to me and you have looked me in the eye.' I do not know what happened to that man but I shall always be grateful to him for God used him to affirm to me two of the most important gifts a Christian should cultivate, a listening ear and a direct eye.

We were in Loret de Mar, known as Sin City – a reputation gained through the activities of young British yobos who came out to enjoy wine, women and song. The hotel managers hoped we might have an influence for good in the place.

We were a mixed bunch, a team struggling with various tensions. One evening we came together for our usual time of worship and there was no sense of unity. Trying to sing, 'Seek ye first the Kingdom of God' was more like a funeral dirge than a desire for God's Kingdom. We knew the mood was not conducive to effective evangelism in the hotels and this was confirmed later from the reports of those who went out. Three of us decided to take the car to a quiet place to pray. As we talked and prayed, we knew God was saying one thing: 'Get the barriers down.' We shared this at breakfast the next morning and the barriers certainly came tumbling down!

One young man thought he was joining a team of young people and I met him at the bus stop. Another young man admitted he had recently been converted to Christianity, he had come off drugs but was still struggling with smoking. His pastor told him that if cigarettes were still a problem he should not be joining an evangelistic team. He was, therefore, going off to a secret place to smoke.

One by one we confessed our contributions to the barrier, asked forgiveness of one another and went off to seal our unity with a game of cricket on the beach. It was a wonderful release and change. Worship came alive and we could once again go out and witness to the love of God. This was a lesson I have never forgotten: Barriers up, worship suffers, witness is ineffective, . . . 'Get the barriers down.'

Purpose Holidays changed over the years in physical terms. From tent to caravan, from caravan to self-catering apartments, the latter with teams of Cambridge students (quite an experience for me!), the mission remained the same: sharing our faith in the hotels. It must be obvious to anyone that those five years of summer outreach made a deep and lasting impression upon me as a person and for my spiritual growth. It is difficult to sum it up in a nutshell but I think Paul's prayer for Philemon would be perfect: 'I pray that you may be active in sharing your faith, so that you will have a full understanding of every good thing we have in Christ.' (Philemon v6) My understanding of the good things grew and the sharing of my faith was to take some new twists and turns.

Evangelist 'team' camping in Spain

New Challenges

I am never quite sure how I became involved with Intercessors for Britain but it was probably because of my friendship with Diana who was the Housekeeper at Ashburnham Christian Conference Centre in Sussex. On return from Purpose Holidays, I would spend some days with her sorting out camping equipment, at the same time improving my saucepan-washing and potato-peeling skills in the centre's kitchen.

These skills were used for the benefit of those attending the yearly 'Intercessors for Britain' conference. We managed to hear some of the excellent talks and somewhere along the line I was challenged to covenant an hour a week to pray for the nation. I have never felt a particular call or gift to intercession; it was always a struggle to maintain my weekly prayer hour. Looking back, I can see how God used this involvement for two very different reasons: first to affirm in me a truth that needed to go from my head to my heart. Secondly to bring me in contact with someone who not only became a friend but played a vital part in God's plan of equipping me for the future.

Denis Clarke, the leader and originator of 'Intercessors for Britain' together with a small team of speakers was heading up a two week course on Bible Meditation to which Diana and I decided to go. They turned out to be two of the most difficult weeks of my life. The teaching was excellent but I felt a total failure until the last day.

We were only allowed to use the authorised version of the Bible. The key word was 'meditation' – allowing God to speak by his Holy Spirit through a verse or given verses which we could cross-reference to other parts of scripture. In the sharing times a wealth of meaningful thoughts came out: God speaking to his people.

I heard nothing, saw nothing, experienced nothing and became more and more depressed and angry. On the last day the cross-references to the verses we were given led me to Psalm 45 and there I read 'Listen, O daughter, consider and give ear; forget your people and your father's house. *The King is enthralled by your beauty;* honour him, for he is your Lord. (Ps 45 v10&11)

Two of the most depressing weeks of my life were transformed into one of the best days of my life as God's truth about me dropped from my head to my heart – where it remains. My Bible reminds me of it as I have written in the margin 'That's me!'

The Church Pastoral Aid Society had area representatives based in Cambridge one of whom was particularly concerned with 'Women's Action' teaching and encouraging women in the church. When Margaret Corstorphine came to Cambridge to head up the women's work her predecessor introduced me to her as a keen 'Intercessor for Britain.' I was still struggling on my own and was delighted when she suggested we got together with one or two others to form a group.

After a few weeks of getting to know one another Margaret asked me if I would like to go with her to a women's meeting in Oxford and lead a workshop. I had to admit my ignorance and ask, 'What is a workshop?' The outcome was an initiation group, the subject being 'Prayer' with Margaret leading and me learning. Since that time I have headed up and been a participant in many workshops and consider they are one of the very best media for learning. They give people the opportunity to air their views, express their doubts, share their testimony, learn from teaching and discover gifts, for example through a drama or dance workshop.

That first invitation was the beginning of a very challenging time for me as Margaret encouraged me not only to lead more workshops but also to be the speaker for a whole day on such subjects as 'Freedom from Fear' and 'Loneliness' subjects to which women could easily relate. Through my own counselling and involvement with the Wholeness Through Christ ministry, I felt I had something positive to share on these things, especially on fear; – I had accumulated a good collection of fears in my *house*. It is some years now since I asked Jesus to re-build His house within my life and to be my landlord.

I have had my ups and downs and have not always done as the Lord has told me. In spite of this He has been wonderfully patient with me. I've been so aware of His love and have drawn much closer to Him. One of the things which impresses me most about Jesus is that He never seems to get tired of putting right my never-ending succession of fears, doubts and failures. He has healed so many of the hurts and resentments, some of which stretched right back beyond my memory.

I must say I have told Jesus quite plainly at times it is very uncomfortable having the beam of His searchlight picking out things in my life that I prefer to keep hidden. Every time I complain, He just looks at me with those indescribably loving eyes and says, 'I am only answering the prayer you pray so often: 'Spirit of the living God, fall afresh on me, take me, break me, mould me . . .' He goes on to say with such compassion in His voice 'This is a prayer I love to hear, I so long to forgive you and free you from all those hidden resentments and fears and hurts which you hold on to. I came that you might have life and have it more abundantly. You cannot know the true abundance of the life I give you until you let me clear out all the clutter and rubbish which you have stored inside you for years.'

I have always felt ashamed after I have complained because every time I have let Jesus clear out some rubbish, I know so wonderfully the truth of His words: 'If the Son sets you free, you will be free indeed.' This became especially true for me when I began to realise what an enormous part fears of all kinds played in my life and how extremely crippling they were.

One day I was sitting reading the story of Peter stepping out of the boat to meet Jesus walking on the water. It was a very familiar passage and normally I identified myself with Peter, with my going out in faith then taking my eyes away from the Lord and being enveloped by the waves. This time it was different; I could see myself sitting in the boat with some of my friends and fellow Christians. The one thing that bound us together at that moment was fear. My own fear was terrifying and all I could hear was my own voice shrieking louder than anyone else's, 'Lord save me.' Suddenly through the noise of the wind I heard the voice of Jesus saying so clearly, 'Take heart, it is I, have no fear.' I immediately stopped shrieking, but there was no inner peace or calm; instead forgetting everyone around me, I found myself saying things to Jesus I had never dared to say before. I said, 'Lord, I am sick and tired of being afraid, you say your perfect love casts out fear, well it has not done so for me. I am afraid of death, afraid of leaving all that is familiar and secure, afraid of what other people think . . .' and so I went on with all my fears tumbling out one after the other until I was exhausted.　By this time we were back in the reality of the house instead of the boat.

Jesus said nothing for while, but in the silence I felt the strangest sense of stillness and calm creep over me. At the same time I felt utterly ashamed at having confessed to so much weakness. I rather haltingly confessed my shame to Jesus and could not bring myself to look at Him. After a moment I felt His arms go around me and to my amazement as I looked up I saw and heard real joy in His face and voice as He said, 'This is the moment I've been waiting for a long time, this moment when you have been willing to voice your fears and cry out to me for help.' I could hardly believe my ears. I had always felt as a Christian I should not have any fears so I had either swept them under the carpet where they could not be seen or pretended they were not there. Jesus must have known what I was thinking because He said, 'There is nothing to be ashamed of in knowing fears. Many of them are there through no fault of your own but stem from the bruises and wounds of life. The sadness is when you hold on to them and do not let me heal them.' Jesus went on, 'If you are crippled and bound in this way you cannot experience the glorious liberty of a child of God and you miss so much of the fullness of joy which I can use through you to attract others into my Kingdom.'

Again we sat quietly for a while. I was pondering on the understanding of Jesus. I had never imagined Him as being afraid of anything and yet I had the feeling that in some inexplicable way He shared my fears with me, not only at this present time but right back to the moment when they had first taken root in my mind. As I was wondering if this could really be true, realising that Jesus knew exactly how I had been feeling over the years, I heard so clearly a small inner voice saying, 'We have not a High Priest who is unable to sympathise with our weaknesses, but one who in every respect has been tempted as we are, yet without sinning.' As the voice faded I suddenly saw three pictures take shape before my eyes. One was of Jesus on top of a high mountain in the wilderness, alone with the devil. The next was of Jesus standing before Pilate with the crowds jeering and mocking. Finally I saw Jesus kneeling in agony of mind and spirit in the garden of Gethsemane with the disciples asleep nearby. The picture remained for some moments and then I heard the voice of Jesus say, 'Do you think I did not fear to leave the security of home to face Satan's attack in the wilderness?' 'Do you think I did not fear what men thought of me and would do to me when I stood before Pilate despised and reviled?' 'Do you think I did not fear death when I knelt alone in the garden of Gethsemane and realised the kind of death that awaited me?'

There was total darkness while Jesus was speaking and then I was aware that right in the centre of the blackness there was a glow of light, which as it grew brighter revealed the stark figure of a broken tortured body hanging on a cross. I stood alone gazing at the man who hung there and was completely transfixed by the most extra-ordinary sensation which came over me. It was as if everything that was un-Christ-like within me, together with all the fears, the hurts and the sorrows of a lifetime were being drawn from me and taken into that body at which I was looking. As the feeling left me I could see there was some writing above the cross, which said, 'He has borne your grief, He has carried your sorrows, He was wounded for your transgressions, He was bruised for your iniquities and with His stripes you are healed.' The truth swept over me together with a new realisation that it was only possible for Jesus to die for us and for our old selves to be crucified with Him because, while He was the Son of God, yet during His life on earth, though sinless, He became totally human and shared that humanity with us. At this point I was aware again that I was in the house and Jesus was sitting beside me smiling. I felt very emotionally drained and did not feel I could talk any more. There was only one thing I wanted to do and I knelt down at Jesus's feet and said, 'Lord, thank you that you were so human. Thank you that you knew what it was to be afraid. Thank you that you accept me just as I am. Thank you that you want to make me just like you. Lord, show me those areas in my life which are still bound by fear and Lord, help me to face them as you did.'

As I finished praying, I felt Jesus' hand on my head and very gently He said, 'You have taken the first step, the way will be long and it will not be easy. There will be work which only you can do and there will be work which only I can do, but the day will come when you will say with victory in your heart, 'I sought the Lord, and He answered me and delivered me from all my fears.'

Before retirement, my public speaking was limited to taking a post-natal class or one for those with bad backs in a physiotherapy department. My first effort at giving personal testimony to a congregation of six elderly ladies in a tin chapel sent me into a flat spin for the whole week before and I feared a near nervous breakdown at the evening service!

No one could claim that I had a gift for public speaking but it is amazing what God can do! I have proved time and time again that 'The one who calls you is faithful and he will do it' (1 Thess 5v24) but I must know I am called otherwise I cannot expect him to do it!

In retrospect these first years of retirement could be summed up in one word: 'Learning.' Learning more of the Bible, learning more about community, learning through public speaking, learning more about the healing ministry, learning through evangelism and most importantly learning more about God. As well as Purpose Holidays which were summer activities, I became involved with an equally scary style of evangelism.

Daniel Cozens came to Holy Trinity Cambridge where Michael Rees was the Vicar, to take up a new appointment as The Dick Rees Missioner. Daniel was, and is, a very gifted evangelist and it was my privilege to be a part of his team on many occasions. We would spend a few days with a church or group of churches encouraging the members to look afresh at their own faith, at the same time being concerned for outreach in their community. This was done through house meetings, community events, visiting, services and anything else that was appropriate and planned by the church in their area. Missions varied considerably and some were a very hard grind bearing seemingly little fruit. At other times there was a positive response with a real sense of anticipation and expectation that God was going to do great things.

It was not only those to whom the mission was directed who experienced God's touch; team members were not left out; I was not left out! Details of most of the missions I went on have faded with time but the mission to March in Cambridgeshire will never be forgotten, mainly because of one small incident which changed my life.

I was out visiting one day and called on an elderly lady who was single and felt neglected by the church. In some ways, I could see why the people were not responding to her needs. She was not the most cheerful of souls. Having said that, she was just echoing the voice of many single people who say 'The church is not interested in single people, only families.'

On completing the visit I returned to the vicarage and happened to meet the vicar in the hall. The poor man was somewhat taken aback when instead of a cheerful greeting he received a broadside as I blurted out with some force, 'I am sick and tired of married people.' I think we both laughed but the outcome from a very enlightened vicar was an invitation for me to come and talk to his congregation on the subject of 'Singleness.' This was a challenge indeed!

That short outburst in the vicarage heralded the beginning of an entirely new challenge on the journey. As I began to think about that first talk for the evening service two things became clear, the first that I should give personal testimony rather than speaking objectively and the second the realization that God had been preparing me for years to bring me to this point in time. In regard to the first, this was to become the pattern for future years. It became increasingly obvious that I was being called to share from my own experiences, always remembering to be biblically based. On looking back, it seemed to be a confirmation of a word I believe I received from God during a communion service earlier:

'Praise be to the God and Father of our Lord Jesus Christ, the Father of compassion and the God of all comfort, who comforts us in all our troubles so that we can comfort those in trouble with the comfort we ourselves have received from God.' (2 Cor 1 v 3.4) One thing was fairly obvious: I could not give a testimony unless I had one to give!

This was no problem; I knew I had so much to share of my struggles in singleness and God's love and healing but the problem was having the courage to do it. I believed the only way was to be honest and open and that would mean exposing my innermost being in public, which was not easy. I had to know without a doubt that this was God's call and had to rely entirely on the Holy Spirit.

I have not kept a copy of that first talk so cannot remember the length or exact content. What still stands out in my memory is the remark made by a young girl at the end of the service. She said, 'You may like to know that as you finished your talk I was left with Jesus, not with you.' She could not have said anything more encouraging. This has always been my aim in speaking or writing: praying that what begins by focusing on me will always end by focusing on Jesus.

As you read my testimony this is my prayer.

The staff, Holy Trinity Cambridge, 1983. Myself next to Michael Rees, front row.

One Way - Single

My pathway through singleness has probably been the most difficult part of my journey: no instant solutions, a long haul but one I would not have changed in any way because I have learned the truth that pain and growth go together. Paul expresses it well in Romans 5, v3&4. '. . .we also rejoice in our sufferings, because we know that suffering produces perseverance, perseverance character; and character hope.' Only when looking back have I seen the true picture.

I was twenty years old when the Second World War broke out in 1939, which meant that I was brought up in a very different climate from this present age. My testimony has to be seen against that background and I looked at it in relation to four areas. Society, the Church, my individual response and relationship with God.

The view of Society in general made it quite clear that to be married conveyed superior status and singleness was second best. There seemed to be little difference in the thinking of the church with its concentration on the nuclear family rather that the Christian family. My individual response to these attitudes in terms of feelings were obviously influenced at the same time by my personality, background and circumstances. My relationship with God was of prime importance, without Him the story would have been very different.

As I said earlier in this book I grew up assuming I would get married and this is what I wanted. I had my romantic dreams: a tall, fair, good-looking husband, a romantic wedding day and honeymoon, a totally idealised view of marriage.

All my natural instincts and desires went along with society's view that marriage should be the primary aim for a young person, the seal of success and the supreme attainment. I agreed, and failure to achieve this did not enter into my thinking.

At the age of twenty-four which, I had decided was the right age for marriage, we were in the middle of World War II when millions of young men were killed or disabled for life. I remember a conversation I had with a friend at that time when we agreed that if we did not get married we would say, 'My fiancé was killed during the war.' This was said jokingly but for me it was serious; it would have given me some status.

I think this was the period when the negatives began to creep in. When I was working at Botleys Park War Hospital I met plenty of men but never achieved a satisfactory relationship. I always felt hurt and rejected. I was not the hit I would have liked to be with the opposite sex. I felt unattractive and a failure as a woman. I blamed my size: I was too tall and my feet were too big.

I never gave up hope but as time went by the feelings of being inferior and second class increased especially if asked, 'When are you going to get married?' or 'Why are you not married?' There was no answer to the first question. But to admit to the truth to the second was far too self exposing and hurtful and it was a very long time before I could admit to the fact that no man had loved me enough to want to marry me.

Society's labels at that time did not help, 'On the shelf,' 'Old maid,' 'Unclaimed treasure,' in other words you've missed the boat. I suppose it was natural that I should ask myself, 'Why? Why? Why? – Is there something wrong with me? Do other people think there is something wrong with me? Why has not someone wanted to marry me?'

I found it difficult to share these feelings with friends, so I secretly took myself off to a psychiatrist. He assured me I was quite normal which was a great relief but did not solve the problem. Apart from the feelings there were certain other difficulties, for instance in the company of an affectionate married couple or alone on social occasions particularly weddings, all of which accentuated my singleness.

I loved ballroom dancing but dances were not always easy. Trying not to look like a wallflower as I sat waiting in the hope that someone would ask me to dance or wishing that I had not tried to look glamorous and worn flatter shoes. It was interesting to see the expressions of those who invited me on to the dance floor but had not realized while I was sitting down that I was six feet tall when standing. Thereby hangs the tale of one man who had the opposite problem from mine.

The Newmarket Hospital Ball was going with a swing when it was announced that the next dance would be a 'Paul Jones', a dance starting with the men going round in a circle in one direction and the ladies the opposite way. Then, when the music stopped you danced with the nearest partner. The inevitable happened. The first time round I came face (not exactly) to face with a pint-sized jockey, who took one look at me and ran on. Unbelievably we met again on the second round, this time he grabbed me round the waist and as the band struck up with the tune 'I'm in the mood for love', he looked up from my chest and said, 'Not quite appropriate is it!' It was even less appropriate when the dance demanded the ladies to go underneath the raised arm of their partner. I ended up on my hands and knees.Here endeth the tale of little and large!

It is important to say at this stage that many of the feelings and reactions I have expressed were not fully acknowledged and accepted by me until I was willing for them to be exposed to the light.

Fortunately I was determined to enjoy life whatever my status, therefore as far as possible I buried all the negative emotions and to most people gave the impression of someone who had no problems at all with singleness. Much of the time this was true. I loved my job, had lots of interests and many friends, both married and single, and enjoyed the freedom of someone who could make her own choices. Buying a flat and having my own home helped a great deal.

When I became a committed Christian I was soon very involved in church activities, but at the same time tried hard to bend God to my will. One particular Bible verse gave me great hope, I discovered, 'if I delighted in the Lord he would give me the desires of my heart' (Ps 37 v4). I think I would describe that as bending the scriptures!

Before too long it was obvious that my 'bending' tactics were not producing the required result, nor were my own efforts. I was in my early fifties and at last had faced the reality that I might not get married. Prayer had not worked, God had not come up with the goods and my final fling at joining a dating agency, known in those days as a marriage bureau, was not a success. in fact it almost made me thankful to be single.

It was not easy to sink my pride but I knew the only way was to come back to God in submission, not demand. Another life-changing moment. I said 'Lord, you win, I am willing to be single, or married; your will be done.' An about-turn in more ways than one. I had come to my senses and experienced the lifting of an enormous burden.

This was only the beginning; there was work to be done. Some things only I could do, some things only God could do.

I had to get beneath the confident, successful 'I can cope' physiotherapist, remove the overcoat as it were and take a look at the underwear which had been on for a long time and needed changing! Everything had to be laid bare before God; everything had to come to the cross of Jesus.

First of all I had to take stock and carefully look at the neglected underwear. I realised my motives for marriage were mainly to meet my needs. I wanted the status and the security of someone to look after me – and, of course, sex - of which incidentally I would have been terrified! I had to admit to all my feelings of anger at society, the church, and married people for their attitudes towards single ones. I had to face my poor self-image and the feelings of inferiority and being a failure. I had to tell God I was not pleased with Him because he had created me too big and therefore unattractive.

Having laid bare all the negatives, the first positive step was to come to the cross in repentance and ask God's forgiveness for all my wrong motives, wrong attitudes and for my anger, resentment and self-pity as well as the lies I believed about myself. Then of course came the harder part of forgiving the individuals, society, the church – even God. Receiving God's forgiveness and forgiving myself was a very important second step to bring the release I needed from all the guilt.

The third positive step was to bring to Jesus all the hurts, the feelings and the lies I believed about myself to receive His healing and begin to take on board the truth about who I was in Christ. The healing and the acceptance of the truth did not happen in five minutes but over a long period of time, mainly through personal prayer, counselling and the promises of scripture which I knew were God's special gifts to me. I remember during a prayer time one morning being completely bowled over by part of Psalm 139. 'For you created my inmost being; you knit me together in my mother's womb. I praise you because I am fearfully and wonderfully made, your works are wonderful, I know that full well.' Suddenly I did know it 'full well.' I had probably read the psalm numerous times but here was the truth which at last I could believe.

The Holy Spirit began to show me deep down that God had created me for himself and there was nothing wrong with what He had made. I could thank the Lord for my body, size and all, and the fact that He actually wanted a girl, not the boy I always longed to be as a child.

The next gift came when I was feeling very low. My morning reading was from Is 43 'I who created you, I who formed you, I who redeemed you, I who called you . . .since you are precious and honoured in my sight and because I love you.' God loved me just as I was. I am wonderfully made, I am loved and God said to me through Is 41 'You are my servant, I have chosen you and have not rejected you.' This was a deeply healing gift. As a single person, I may not have been chosen by a man. I may have been rejected by many men but God has chosen me and God will never reject me. What a promise. What a truth.

At one time I held the world's view that as a single person I am not fulfilled, I am incomplete, only half a person. This, of course, is saying also that Jesus was unfulfilled, only half a person. In fact, of course, He was the only complete person who ever lived. I am so thankful He was single.Over the years I have learned that Jesus is the only one who can satisfy my deepest needs, no human being can do this, no husband, parent, friend, child; only in Christ can I be complete and truly fulfilled.

My status is as a child of God – not in marriage, ministry, my gifts, or anything else. My security is with Jesus, the one who has promised me eternal life. I know without doubt it's okay to be single, it's okay to be me, it's okay to be a woman. I am equal in value to every member of the body of Christ and equally loved.

In 1981 a friend invited me to talk about singleness to the Christian Institute in Cambridge. We arranged that Michael, a single man, would give the biblical background and I would follow with personal testimony. I believe it was a 'God incidence' that in the audience that night there was a member of the Christian Friendship Fellowship (CFF) a pioneer, nationwide, now worldwide organisation which through local groups, holidays and conferences has done so much to help single people of every status to feel accepted, find friendship and sometimes a marriage partner. My testimony was taped and taken by this unknown lady to the National Easter Conference of CFF where it was played to the assembled company. I knew nothing about this but it resulted in my being invited to speak at several of their events, both local and national.

Following on CFF I became involved with 'Network' an organisation with similar aims run by David and Gill Ruffle. They have a real concern for the single person and their ministry and teaching continues to be an encouragement to thousands. I loved working with them and over a period of many years it has been a very rewarding experience for me to share with them and help at their New Year house parties.

As time went on, I was to realize more and more how true it was that 'what I give to God he takes, and what he takes he uses.' One of the major struggles of my life had been to do with singleness but God kept handing me the greatest privilege in enabling me to share with so many single people what He had done, and was continuing to do in my life and what He could do and wanted to do for every hurting single person.

I had always thought it important to emphasize that I could only speak as me with my personality, my background, my circumstances and the social boundaries of my upbringing, as well as the fact that I had never been married. Divorced, widowed and single parents would have their own particular needs but there was much I could address which would be common to us all – even the married!

The subjects I tackled were many and varied: friendship, loneliness, living for today, sexuality, forgiveness, choosing life. It was of primary importance to base every talk on biblical teaching and, even if talking about myself, to point everyone to Jesus.

As time went on I could hardly believe that this was me, the one who was not eloquent or used to speaking publicly, the one who disliked studying and having to spend hours in preparation, the one who did not want to stay single, but said she was content. God was moving in very mysterious ways. In relation to contentment one of the fallacies when sharing my testimony with single people was to give the impression that I had got it all together and never again would there be a problem.

Today I know what I said then was true, there would always be times when the wrong attitudes, the disappointed hopes, the 'if only's and the acute sense of loss would raise their heads. Even at the age of eighty-two, as I am now, I do not consider it abnormal for some of the negatives to surface occasionally. In fact I think they are an indication that I am human and still alive, and for that I am thankful.

Fortunately with time I have learned how to get back into the positive – 'Give thanks with a grateful heart.' One of the great advantages of being single is the freedom it gives to come, to go, to say yes or no, but at the same time it means to be without excuse when in another of His mysterious ways God presents an open door!

CHAPTER 14

Invitation to Lee Abbey

Each year during the Easter vacation students from Oxford and Cambridge were invited to Lee Abbey, with reduced fees, in order to spend their mornings working on the estate, clearing paths, painting fences, planting trees or do whatever else needed doing in springtime. Afternoons would be given to leisure activities and evenings to teaching.

It was in 1980 after Patsy Evans (now Kettle) our chaplain to the students had left Cambridge that Peter Judd the chaplain to Clare College invited me to fill the gap. He wanted me to organise some of the arrangements and go down to Lee Abbey to help pastorally with the students. I was, to say the least, surprised, was nervous and very aware of the age gap. I was still learning the lesson that 'The one who calls you is faithful and He will do it.' I loved being back at Lee Abbey, enjoyed the whole week, even the students, and God had more in store!

'Here I am Lord, do with me what you will, send me where you will, but please not to speak to a youth group.' Nick and Liz Manning, the leaders of our Church Youth Group in Cambridge, asked me if I would be the speaker at their summer house party for which they had booked the beach chalet at Lee Abbey. My immediate reaction was to say 'no, I do not know how to relate, never mind speak to a bunch of teenagers.' Nick and Liz were so insistent that I was the right person and saying 'yes' meant I would be at Lee Abbey three times during the year having also booked in as a guest.

The preparation for the houseparty took hours and hours, amongst other things I decided to talk on doubts and fears and I had plenty of both. After the first talk Nick came to me and said, 'Give more personal testimony. That's what they will respond to.' How right he was. Most of my preparation through sweat and tears went out of the window and I spent a whole afternoon re-hashing everything. To my amazement I got through the week and the teenagers were great, we *did* 'relate!'

The following year, in September 1981, Patsy, who was now working in a church in Woking, was invited to go as speaker to Lee Abbey. She was nervous at the thought and asked me to go as a guest to support her. Whatever was happening? This would be my fourth visit to Lee Abbey in two years having been on a second working party in the spring with Jane Keiller, Patsy's successor.

I was quite happy at the thought of another holiday there especially to support Patsy who had always been a support and encouragement to me in Cambridge especially when I was going through my post-retirement identity crisis; we had also become very good friends.

Looking back, I can see God's hand in it all so clearly. There was some conflict in my mind because Daniel Cozens was running a mission in Jersey during that same week and I would have loved to be there. Fortunately, Patsy's invitation came first, and I accepted it, not for a single minute suspecting that the next invitation would turn my life upside down.

It was the first night of the house party. Supper was over, music was playing and guests were being encouraged to join in with the folk dancing, one of Lee Abbey's long held traditions. I was in the canteen area in conversation with Gay Perry over a cup of coffee. I was about to go in and join the dancers when John Perry, the warden of Lee Abbey came and joined us and immediately asked me if I would be willing to come and help in a pastoral capacity at the New Year house party. Two older members of the community were retiring and there was a gap. They needed some mature people to off-set the young age of the majority of community members. John realised that he could not employ retired people but there would be those who could give time without pay and just receive their keep.

I think I was the first and to put it mildly was gob-smacked at such an unexpected invitation. At the same time I was excited, with a real conviction that this was the work of the Holy Spirit, so how could I refuse? I said 'yes' and added 'Christmas as well!' It was understood that this would be a trial run on both sides not knowing quite how it would work out for either of us. There were many surprises ahead.

I drove down that first Christmas in fear and trembling, not knowing what to expect, feeling very unsure of myself. I was shown to a lovely room at the top of the house with a glorious view of the bay. It had just been vacated by a chaplain and all that was left was a bed in the bedroom, a table and two chairs in the sitting room. Somehow, it did not seem empty because there was a lovely welcome card, a large bowl of fruit and a bouquet of flowers – a Lee Abbey speciality.

I could not help asking myself, 'what am I doing here? Am I a guest or a member of the community? What happens if no-one wants to talk and pray with me?' All I could do was to say 'Lord here I am, I believe you have sent me here, over to you.'

The first morning at breakfast I sat next to a lady who very quickly started to pour out her troubles and I asked her if she would like me to pray with her; thankfully she said 'yes.' I truly believed that this was God's confirmation that I was in the right place at the right time. Not many people poured out their troubles to me at breakfast over the next twelve years!

The experiment seemed to work on both sides and John asked me to come back for a month in the summer. For the next two years I commuted from Cambridge to Lee Abbey for increasing periods of time. In between visits to Lee Abbey I became very involved helping Jane with student activities. I was still on the staff at Holy Trinity and for good measure went on the occasional mission with Daniel and W.T.C. courses. Suddenly it all became too much. I seemed to spend my time packing and unpacking, driving to and fro, always missing something either end. Decision time had come.

My heart was at Lee Abbey but I did not know if I could stand the pace full-time and more importantly, I had no idea if it would even be considered. I sounded out the idea with Priscilla Hamel-Cooke, one of the chaplains who was very positive. It was taken to the warden/chaplains meeting where it had a unanimous response: 'Yes!'

I was to let my flat in Cambridge, make my home at Lee Abbey and become a full member of community. I was still a volunteer and this meant I would not have to abide by restricted holidays. Without this freedom to be away more frequently, I am sure that I would not have lasted a year, never mind ten! I had one proviso before I could leave my home and move down to Lee Abbey. I had to have a larger room.

Accommodation had always been a problem at Lee Abbey with an increasing demand for more guest rooms and a growing community. I had to be fitted in often for a month or two at a time. In the early days I flitted from pillar to post but eventually acquired my own space, not quite as large as the good-sized flat in which I normally lived. I did not find it too easy to sleep, be at leisure and work, all in a room 6ft x 6ft, though I felt I had been well prepared for such an eventuality during my bed-sitting room days.

I remember driving down on one visit saying to the Lord 'If this is to be my room from now on I will accept it as your will.' I knew Lee Abbey was concerned for me but it was the best they could do and certainly it had its lighter moments.

One of Lee Abbey's activities is to invite groups of guests to have after-dinner coffee with community in their rooms which enables them to see some of the accommodation and find out what life is like living on community. For one coffee group I invited five people into my space, four on the bed, one on the chair and me on the floor. I did not know quite how to reply when one dear lady exclaimed 'Oh what a dear little room' She had obviously not seen me trying to pray with somebody and lay hands on them as we sat side by side on the bed!

I did move to a larger room and as the years went by progressed gradually up the scale in size and outlook. I eventually ended up with the most beautiful view in the house, a log fire and, most exciting of all, my own bathroom. This was the height of bliss but a long way ahead in this story.

An unexpected invitation came which would take me journeying far afield.

South Africa

The Cape of Good Hope, near Cape Town

A friend in Cambridge phoned me one day and told me a friend of her's, Mona Eastwick, was coming over from South Africa and wanted to rent a cottage for two months in the summer, did I know of anywhere suitable? Yes, I did not own a cottage but she could have my flat while I was down at Lee Abbey.

I did not meet Mona but talked to her on the telephone and before she left she said 'Do come and see me in Cape Town if you ever visit South Africa.' I casually shared this with Steve and Sue Hobbs who had come over for the summer to do youth work and were shortly returning to South Africa. The response was short and to the point 'Why not come?'

Soon after their return, Steve sent me a detailed itinerary of what I could do on a six week trip. It would take me from Cape Town to Johannesburg and everywhere else in between! He asked for an answer by December so that he could make the necessary bookings for coaches, game parks, mountain huts. . . .This was an amazing opportunity especially as I thought Australia would be the end of my long-haul travel. I had never envisaged anything so exciting and expensive in retirement. I was longing to go but very concerned at the thought of spending so much money on myself.

Once again I had reckoned without God. I was praying with a friend one day and we had lapsed into silence. South Africa must have been in my thoughts because I had a real conviction that God was saying 'Sheila, the money is mine not yours and if I choose to send you to South Africa – go!'

The experience was unforgettable. I was there at the height of apartheid and in a year of severe drought. Travelling through the country I was able to see so many sides of South Africa: the incredible beauty of the Drakensberg mountains and the Eastern Transvaal, the wildlife of the game parks and the stark contrast of Soweto, the African township outside Johannesburg. One of the most interesting experiences was visiting a school for African children where a pioneer feeding scheme was in operation.

I met so many people but Mona and Steve and Sue in particular, by the places we visited, tried to give me a picture of both the glories and agonies of their country. This was the first time I had travelled abroad without a companion and before leaving England had asked friends to pray specifically for a six-day bus journey from Cape Town to Durban, along the Garden Route, when I would be on my own. If I had known beforehand what was going to happen I might have looked for a different means of transport!

For the first four days I was in a forty-five seater coach with the driver and a very keen, pro-apartheid, Dutch reformed family consisting of grandmother, mother and daughter. They departed at Port Elizabeth and for the next two days the driver and I kept each other company!

The interesting part was - I took it in my stride, was not scared though very pleased to see my friends in Durban!

After visiting Johannesburg and the Kruger National Park I flew back to England and Lee Abbey with a few hundred slides with which I was able to share my experiences many times.

I was starting another new phase on The Journey.

Sheila with African Children in the Drakensberg mountains

Lee Abbey - Part of the Community

A year or so before I started to help at Lee Abbey, Roger Davies, a friend, had said to me 'I can see you on the Lee Abbey Community.' My instinctive reply was 'no way, I could not stand it!'

Roger was right and here I was on the community as a full-time member of the pastoral team. This was now my home, I had no idea for how long, but these were to be the most challenging years of my life in terms of relationships, demands on time and the discovery of gifts. God had been preparing me for this for many years.

I had had a taster but this was diving in at the deep end. I came to experience with seventy others of different ages, background and nationality what Christian community was all about. I had to learn how to communicate to the wider church through the 6,000 plus guests who visited Lee Abbey each year for conferences and holidays.

It meant worshipping together, working together, playing together and learning together how to cope with the pressures of a busy life, how to face honestly and openly the conflicts, trials and tribulations which inevitably occur with those living together in such close contact. It always seemed that when tensions were at their greatest behind the scenes a guest would say, 'what a wonderful peace there is about the place!' As I settled in to a more permanent existence, I was increasingly aware of what a privilege it was to be called to the Lee Abbey Community with its breadth of life and ministry.

In the early days my main task was to be available to talk and pray with any individual guest or member of community who had a particular concern. Not only did I meet hundreds of interesting people but I also had the immense privilege of playing a small part in the whole ministry of Lee Abbey and God's plan and purpose in changing and transforming the lives of His people.

As I talked and prayed with more and more guests, I realised that forgiveness was not only an issue on nearly every occasion but there was also a tremendous amount of ignorance due to lack of teaching. Years earlier I had experienced the power and release of God' s forgiveness when I felt guilt after my mother's death. Then later I experienced the relief when I made the list under the guidance of the Holy Spirit and brought to the cross all the resentments and anger which had lain hidden for years. I had also learned the importance of forgiveness in the healing of a friendship. Not least in my list were my various landladies whom it took me a long time to forgive but the cellar of my 'house' holds the story.

When I asked Jesus Christ to re-build the house of my life and be the landlord I intended that he should take over all the rooms but somehow this did not happen. I let him have free access downstairs where at any rate to the outsider it looked clean and respectable but I would only allow him an occasional peep at the upstairs rooms because I felt I must keep myself to myself at all times.

At least, this is how I felt until a few months ago when I suddenly became very tired of my own company and knew I needed Jesus to straighten me out. He did. He transformed the rooms I had kept so tightly shut and showed me that He is so much more capable of running my life than I am. It was only a few weeks later that another door had to be unlocked and opened.

I was feeling a bit tense at the time and had been moaning at Jesus because He had not healed a complaint I had which the doctors labelled as 'nervous.' The symptoms had been there for many years and I was so fed up with them that when Jesus said, 'There are some things in your past life which have caused a great deal of tension but you have kept them away from me. Are you prepared to let me deal with them?' I said, 'Yes Lord, I will do anything because this anxiety is not honouring you.' A day or two after this conversation Jesus sent me out to go and talk to a group of people about forgiveness.

I thought this was a good subject, one I knew quite a lot about, so I went off in a pretty smug frame of mind. I enjoyed it and thought the evening a great success. I even came back and told Jesus that one or two of those people really needed to do a bit of forgiving. He said nothing and off I went to bed feeling very pleased with myself.

The next morning I was sitting reading in the book of Acts. I read 'Repent therefore and turn again that your sins may be blotted out, that times of refreshing may come from the presence of the Lord.' My immediate reaction was – 'how well that fits in with those people I was talking to last night.' No sooner had the thought taken shape in my mind than a feeling of shame came over me and I knew perfectly well that the verse was speaking to me. Of course, I quickly dismissed it and hurried on to the rest of the chapter.

When I had finished reading I noticed it was pouring with rain outside; not the kind of day for going out if it could be avoided. I was just pondering on what I should do when I was aware that Jesus was in the room. Although I did not consciously hear Him speak I could have sworn that he said, 'Why not spend the day cleaning up the cellar?' This was a job I never had the will or the courage to tackle and so it got left. It was the junk hole into which I had thrown all the things I did not want to look at and yet had not the heart to get rid of. Occasionally I would go down and look at the mess but would hastily retreat and lock the door because I knew it could be a long and dirty business to clear the place and it was not doing any harm to leave the stuff there – at least that is what I thought.

The rain looked well settled in so against my better judgment I decided to tackle the cellar and changed into old clothes and went down there. As I passed Jesus in the hall He gave me a lovely smile and said, 'I will not come down with you now but call me if you need any help.' I was rather surprised at His concern. I had always made it clear that the cellar was my province and much too dirty for Him to deal with.

My heart seemed to sink in proportion to the number of steps which led down from the passage-way and my spirits did not lift as I turned the key in the lock and opened the door. The damp air hit me, as did the smell of mildew, and the dim light just served to accentuate the cobwebs and the dirt. The whole atmosphere was eerie and depressing. My first reaction was to turn back – I could not face it – but the door had shut firmly behind me.

I paused for a little while to get my eyes accustomed to the dim light and to my horror heard voices; there were obviously other people in the cellar. I was terrified: and as I turned to try and get to the door they surrounded me by holding hands in a circle so that I was trapped in the middle of them.

I tried frantically to break the circle but they stood firm. I could not see their faces but when I realised there was nothing I could do to get out I stood rooted on the spot and gradually became aware that one after the other was speaking and something of what they were saying rang a bell in my mind.

I listened carefully and heard one and then another say,

'We are not interested in you, only your money and your rations;'
'If you cannot come in at the proper time you will be locked out;'
'Take a week' s notice, my husband cannot stand you here any longer;'

'I don' t mind if you are cold, you are not having a fire;'
'You are an immoral lot, you can all get out.'

I could not stand any more and blocked my ears to any further sound. The sudden realisation that they were the landlords and landladies of my past caused a wave of loneliness and hurt and self-pity to come over me and I heard myself calling, *'Lord Jesus please come and help me. I need you so much.'*

Even before I had finished speaking Jesus was beside me and I burst into a flood of tears in His arms. It was such a comfort to feel safe and wanted and I hardly noticed the circle had broken and the people had disappeared. As soon as I had calmed down Jesus led me to a corner where we could sit on a couple of old packing cases and He said, *'Now tell me all about it.'*

The fear in me had died down and this was replaced by all the painful memories that had been pushed down and, I thought, buried in the recesses of my mind. Perhaps for the first time ever I was now completely honest with Jesus and told him exactly what I thought of these people. I started off at length missing not a detail of the wrongs, real and imaginary, which they had inflicted upon me.

I said, *'They are a mean, petty, stupid, lying lot and I hate them all for giving me such a miserable ten years and what's more I never want to see another landlady or landlord for the rest of . . .'* I stopped in mid-sentence, the look on Jesus' face was enough to make me realise what I had said. Again I burst into tears, this time not because of what a landlord had done to me but because of the awful hurt I had caused to the One whom I had especially asked in to be the landlord of my life. The One who had never failed me and who was so completely and utterly loving and perfect.

I felt so dreadful I knelt at Jesus' feet and said, *'Forgive me Lord, I did not mean what I said, you know I love you and want you as my landlord.'* I was quite expecting to know immediate forgiveness from Jesus but it did not come. Instead He said, *'What about your forgiveness?'* I said, *'What do you mean, my forgiveness?'* He sighed as He replied, *'Only the other night you were quoting to your group 'Forgive if you have anything against anyone; so that your Father also in heaven may forgive you your sin.' Now look at yourself. Why should you expect me to forgive you when you have consciously admitted to me that you have so much resentment and bitterness in your heart?'*

As Jesus was talking, the truth really began to dawn and I knew not only that I *had to forgive the wrongs done to me but I needed also to ask forgiveness for my attitude and behaviour towards them.*

I began to wish I had asked Jesus into the cellar long ago. I knew perfectly well it had not done me any good to hang on to all the rubbish. My defences were pretty well down now but I had one more go saying, 'Lord, I cannot possibly forgive them, they hurt me too much and anyway I do not know how.' Fortunately Jesus knew my heart better than I did and said, 'Before we go any further I want to talk to you through the Scriptures and then I shall ask you one question.'

He took me from the fifty-third chapter of Isaiah through to the garden of Gethsemane, to his betrayal and trial, right to the moment when He hung on the cross and said, 'Father, forgive them for they know not what they do.'

My feelings as He talked could not possibly be put into words, the reality of his love and my unworthiness just filled my heart. As never before I could echo the words of the hymn, 'Love so amazing, so divine, demands my soul, my life, my all.' When Jesus asked me the one question: 'Do you forgive them?' I had no hesitation in answering, 'Yes, Lord, I do want to forgive them.'

While I had been sitting listening to Jesus I was quite unaware of what was happening in the cellar and was very surprised on looking up to see what looked like a row of front doors with numbers on them: 49, 7, 32. I recognised the houses as those in which I had lodged many years ago.

Jesus said, 'You are now going to knock on every door and go right inside and say you forgive each person who you feel has hurt or wronged you in any way.' Fear rose up within me and I was about to protest that I could not possibly go in alone when Jesus put His arm round me and added, 'and I shall come in with you.' I knocked at every door and as we met individually those against whom I bore so much resentment, we joined hands with each other and with Jesus and as I said the words, 'I forgive you,' I knew it was His forgiveness flowing through me and that without Him I could have said nothing.

When we left the final house Jesus said, 'It's time to go now.' We walked across the cellar and my eyes were suddenly opened to the complete transformation which had taken place: the cellar was light and clean with no signs of any dirt or cobwebs and all the rubbish had disappeared. As we got to the door I looked back and there were the people; I could see their faces now, they were happy and laughing and waving goodbye.

I was filled with the strangest sensation; for so many years every memory was painful but now all ill feelings had gone and I could only see them as those who had taken me into their homes as a stranger and looked after me and helped to shape me into the person Jesus wanted me to be. I waved back smiling too, I had forgiven them, they had forgiven me and we were friends at last.

I locked the door behind me and gave the key to Jesus. I knew I would never need to go down there again. He was now the landlord of the cellar. We went back into the sitting room for there was one more thing to be done that day. I knelt at Jesus' feet and said, 'Lord, forgive my sin as I have forgiven those who have sinned against me.' There was no doubting his forgiveness this time as he lifted me to my feet and his joy swept away 30 years of bitterness.

As I looked out of the window and saw the rain had stopped, sunlight began to flood the room and I remembered those words:

'Repent therefore and turn again that your sins may be blotted out, that times of refreshing may come from the presence of the Lord.' Acts 3:19

Workshops on all kinds of subjects were often a part of the programme at Lee Abbey and my experience prompted me to offer a workshop on 'Forgiveness.' I was apprehensive at first not knowing how many cans of worms would be spilled out; there were some of course but I look back on this group as one of the best and most encouraging things I ever did at Lee Abbey.

The need was obvious by the numbers who would sign up week after week. The basis was biblical of course, but I tried to help in a practical way and open up discussion on the hows and whys and wherefores instead of just the theory. For example, thinking of some of the reasons why we find it hard to receive God's forgiveness, what prevents us from forgiving ourselves? How can we forgive those who had hurt us so much? I gained immeasurably from these groups both in confidence in leadership but even more importantly in being allowed to share in some of the pain, the questionings and the joys in so many people's lives. I still occasionally have the joy of meeting someone who tells me that as a result of coming to the workshop they have been able to forgive and be forgiven with a consequent healing of relationships. 'To God be the glory.'

One of the aims of these writings is to show how God at every stage of my life has been preparing me for what is to come. In this context, I was so grateful for all the missions I had been on with Daniel Cozens.

Although Lee Abbey's main vision was to bring people to the Centre, a very important part of the work included sending mission teams to any church or group of churches who requested help. Originally these missions were under the leadership of one of the chaplains and later under the leadership of a chaplain/evangelist who was appointed specifically for the task. I was included in several missions even after I came to live in Cirencester when I was invited to join the team from Devon together with one or two other Lee Abbey friends. 'The Friends' are those who commit themselves to support Lee Abbey particularly in prayer and also in giving.

For the young, community missions were a wonderful training ground and for all of us a faith builder. There were many ways of sharing our faith, personal testimony being one of the most powerful. With an essentially young team dance, drama and music played an important part in school assemblies, parish parties and church services.

You could count me out of dance but I so enjoyed letting the years drop off as, dressed in a duvet, I had to act and speak like double cream, one of the ingredients of a cake trying to illustrate church unity! Missions were fun!

One of the very important features of a Lee Abbey mission was the fact that community back home were an integral part of what was going on: praying corporately, praying in partnership with a team member, in constant telephone communication and in sending letters of encouragement. A week or weekend of mission was a real building exercise for the whole of community.

Lee Abbey and the Arts

There is much truth in the saying, 'Laughter is the best medicine.' Certainly working among patients in a physiotherapy department we encouraged fun and laughter to create an atmosphere which would aid recovery, both physical and mental.

At Lee Abbey, I knew laughter also acted as spiritual medicine for the guests and an essential ingredient for community living and working in a spiritual hothouse. Leaving so much laughter behind was a great loss to me when I left Lee Abbey. Amusements were many and varied, guest and community, concerts, Christmas pantomimes, party games and informal absurdities during a meal.

One lunch time it was decided to present a taster of what was to come at the New Year's Eve Ball. As a member of the host team and known as a 're-cycled teenager' I was designated to play the part of Cinderella and was asked to present a preview. After appearing as the poor servant girl who was only fit to sweep the dining room floor, my carriage was brought in the shape of a food trolley. I am not sure if I bounced on it with too much vigor but something happened which caused my head to go down and my legs to go up. The guests gasped, fearing an injury. I was concerned at what might be revealed through my splayed legs! I have no doubt the ugly sisters would have cackled with glee at such an undignified exit.

On the night of the ball all went well. I rode in state on top of the dressed-up trolley-cum-carriage drawn by two community mice and met my handsome prince in the form of John Perry for the first dance!

Straight acting was not my scene but I always enjoyed opportunities to play the fool; certain incidents will never be forgotten. On the last night of family house parties in particular, guests would be encouraged to use their ingenuity and dress to match the chosen theme. It was amazing what some of them concocted out of nothing. We too had to play our part.

One evening the theme was Hawaiian and I, together with some members of the pastoral team, entertained the guests by cavorting around the dining room in a so-called Hawaiian dance. We were all wearing plastic grass skirts bought in Lynton. I think our foolery was much enjoyed.

Hawaiian Dancers at Lee Abbey

My memories go further. To draw the evening to a close Alan Smith, one of the chaplains still dressed in his Hawaiian outfit, stood up to give a short epilogue. I was sitting on the floor, also wearing my plastic grass skirt over a pair of scarlet bloomers which seemed an appropriate undergarment for the occasion. Alan based his talk on the wise and foolish virgins. To this day, I do not know if I heard him correctly but at one point I am sure I heard him say 'Be dressed and ready!' I was very conscious of my attire and can distinctly remember the spontaneous prayer I prayed, 'Lord please do not come now while I am dressed like this. I really cannot go up in scarlet bloomers and a plastic grass skirt!' Fortunately my prayer was answered, He did not come!

So my parts included the Hawaiian dancer, Cinderella, and then my favourite character of all, the mute lady who could only communicate by using facial contortions. She was created originally as a last-minute unrehearsed offering at a Community Christmas Concert in duet with Audrey Martin-Doyle, one of the chaplains. Audrey spoke aloud whatever came into her head, the first occasion to portray how the people of Lynton might regard the goings-on at Lee Abbey. I responded with varying appropriate facial expressions. The act was enjoyed so much it even found its way into a pantomime. A special appearance for me was on 'Blind Date,' when dressed in the usual tweed coat and woolly hat with carrots and leeks hanging out of my basket, I hoped that I would choose the right man to fly with me to an exotic destination. You should have seen the three choices!

One of the Lee Abbey traditions is to have an evening of folk dancing which I always enjoyed. One evening, having exhausted myself I stood apart talking to a guest. I was not sure how to take it when she said, "My husband has just said of you 'My, she' s a game old bird'" - I think I quite liked that!

In a similar vein one of my most treasured possessions, now hanging on my kitchen door, is a plaque left on my desk by two young members of community which says, 'I am not an OAP, I am a re-cycled teenager.' What a gift!

Music has always been an important part of my life. I could not sing a solo but did so enjoy singing with the Granta Singers in Cambridge. Fortunately there was no such thing as an audition at Lee Abbey; we had a four-part group which was open to all. We rehearsed once a week mainly for input into the Sunday services. During my time we had the honour of singing in Westminster Abbey for the consecration of John Perry as Bishop of Southampton and also in Coventry Cathedral at the memorial service of Geoffrey Rogers, one of the early much-loved wardens of Lee Abbey.

One cannot imagine Lee Abbey without music; part of the ethos was to bring before the church, through the guests, different forms and styles of worship using both traditional and modern hymns and songs. Music conferences were always popular as were the home-grown music workshops. Community members who had an instrument were encouraged to use it, whatever their standard, and play for worship. I was always amazed how many wrong notes could be covered up by one good pianist or instrumentalist. Hereby hangs a story!

One of the deepest regrets of my life was not having learned to play an instrument. I dabbled with the recorder but my sights were on the clarinet. When I casually shared this ambition with a friend he suggested I talk it over with two girls on Community both of whom played that instrument. The first one said she thought at my age (68 at the time) I would find the breathing too difficult, the second one said 'I will bring my clarinet to your room and you can have a go.'

I did have a go, bought the necessary tutor books and eventually achieved my two ambitions, to play for worship and to be an Aker Bilk playing 'Strangers on the Shore' not with quite the same expertise, but it was fun! I do not think there is anywhere else in the world I could have done this and where my amateur bumblings and squeaks were so acceptable. One friend, on hearing me practice asked me if I had a baby hippo in my room!

Lee Abbey fosters a unique gift of encouragement to those who need it. Most young people (and older ones!) spending time on the Community would testify to the fact that Lee Abbey is a place where, through endless opportunities for expression, gifts of all kinds are discovered, encouraged and used. There would be those coming on Community bringing particular gifts in music, drama or dance. As they shared their enthusiasm and skills through workshops, with serious and light- hearted presentations others involved would find an interest or a gift emerging.

What we called 'Interest Groups,' an evening entertainment for guests, brought forth many gifts from young community members. Craft skills of all kinds, sporting activities and talents for creative writing or poetry reading. You name it, as they shared it somebody would enjoy it. Over the years I saw so many guests go home determined to continue with something creative that they had discovered and enjoyed at Lee Abbey. They too made discoveries of hidden talents and like us found life was full of surprises!

On the more serious side, because community members had opportunities to prepare and lead worship, to organize walks, outings or events, gifts of leadership and organization would be recognized and encouraged as well as gifts of hospitality as they spent time with the guests.

Many young people came straight from school or university and had to work in departments alien to their experience and I know many of them were surprised to find themselves with cooking skills or the ability to bring lambs into the world! I learned one very important fact at Lee Abbey and that is how dependent we are on each other. I may have a gift but I need someone else's and they need mine to bring it to life.

I went to Dave Hopwood, whose gift was in drama and said, "I have a testimony I would like to share. Could you write a short drama to illustrate what I am trying to say?' He wrote 'The Dolls House' which was one of his very best and a much-used sketch on various occasions. Later when I brought slides back from Canada, Jenny Pike, (now Hellyer), our musical director, composed some very moving music which really brought the slides to life.

To a different set of photos Jill Stedman, a pianist and musical director following Jenny, together with Simeon Wood and John Gerighty a flautist and guitarist, who after leaving Lee Abbey were to become a professional duo, composed some lovely music which the guests enjoyed as a live performance. It was such fun doing these things together and I have taken away so many happy memories of these days to enjoy for the rest of my life.

Music at Lee Abbey – Sheila playing the Clarinet

Healing and Pruning

One of the advantages of being on the pastoral team came from opportunities to hear many exceptional speakers. There is one who sticks in my memory from one sentence she spoke. It pointed to an area of my life which I had no idea needed healing.

Ann Long in her talk said, 'Who is on the throne of your life?' The Holy Spirit made it quite clear to me what my answer should be. Ann later talked and prayed with me. I stepped down from the throne, invited Jesus back where He belonged and went into the Chapel where I asked God to show me anything else I needed to know to correct my attitudes.

In my thoughts I went back to my days as a physiotherapist when I found myself telling the Lord angrily that I could not always live up to the expectations of being cheerful, patient and strong. Feelings came tumbling to the surface; some of the resentments I knew were directed rightly or wrongly at the expectations I thought came from patients. I am certain others were directed at my own demands for perfection, which I did not achieve.

On the other side of the coin I was also angry at the way patients put me on a throne because I knew I enjoyed being there! As someone who was so happy in her job and loved the patients I was very surprised at what had been hidden and unacknowledged for so many years.

One of the visual aids I used in my forgiveness workshops was to give each guest a pebble from the beach and suggest that it could be thrown over the cliff into the sea, 300 ft below, as a practical symbol of an intention, desire or a definite decision to forgive and be forgiven for any specific reason. After my morning in the Chapel I decided to take two pebbles out to Jenny's Leap, the cliff-top a short walk from the house, where legend has it that Jenny threw herself over when jilted by her lover on her wedding day.

As I walked out along the path on a November afternoon, I noticed all the dead leaves lying on the ground and the occasional leaf fluttering down from a tree. I remember thinking, 'the tree has to let its leaves fall before new growth can emerge in spring time; this is a picture for me: today something is going to die and God will bring new life.'

The first pebble represented my decision to throw over all my anger and resentment that had surfaced that morning; it went over quite easily. The second pebble was agonisingly difficult. I thought I had put my physiotherapy days successfully behind me and let go of the patients and the responsibility I had held for them. Up to a point this was true but it was the Holy Spirit who revealed that the second pebble represented all the goodbyes I had never faced and the consequent grief, which had been buried and was now bringing tears. I paced up and down crying to the Lord 'I cannot say goodbye, I cannot let my patients go, I love them too much.' I know God was giving me the opportunity to face the problem; it was important for the future and might never come again.

Fortunately there was no one about and eventually I called to mind and pictured the three hospitals where I had been at my happiest and chickened out on the goodbyes. In imagination, I walked into the wards and the physiotherapy departments and aloud to the seagulls and the wind said my farewells, as I should have done years ago.The pebble went over into the sea, with a load of tears, as a symbol that I had let go of my patients, my responsibilities and the grief of all my years as a physiotherapist. The leaves had fallen and almost immediately I knew spring had come. There was healing and there was pruning.

At sixty-plus I was the grandmother of the community and in spite of the fact that I enjoyed being dubbed the 'the recycled teenager,' I did not always find it easy to live with sixty young people, nor they with me. Most of the time there were no problems and I loved living alongside so many young people but every now and again the generation gap became apparent and one incident stands out in my mind which dented my pride considerably.

The guests who came to Lee Abbey are many and varied with ages ranging from babes-in-arms to the ninety-plus. Some house parties and conferences are geared more to families, some to folks with a special interest and others are designed for young people. For obvious reasons, at certain times of year, older people are in the majority.

Being a champion of the elderly I found myself getting very annoyed when I felt that the attitude of young community members towards the elderly was less enthusiastic than mine. I decided I would have to say something when we were all gathered together for morning prayers. As one who preferred sweeping everything difficult under the carpet I was not looking forward to the prospect. What happened was very unexpected.

Before going to prayers I got down on my knees in my room hoping for a mighty revelation from God telling me what to say. Instead I had a mighty revelation from God about myself as He spoke to me and said 'Sheila, what about your attitude towards young people?' I knew exactly what He meant, my less-than-enthusiastic welcome to 120 students on the Oxford working party!

So, I ended up having to go to the chapel and tell the truth about what had happened. I had to ask forgiveness for any wrong attitudes I had towards young people. It was a salutary experience and one I will never forget. I am still learning the lesson that it is good to look at my own attitudes before condemning others. There was even more pruning to come.

As a member of the pastoral team, I was fortunate in that, apart from community commitments, my time was spent with guests. Every now and again the role changed and in turn I took my place on the team together with one person drawn from each department who planned and hosted the conference or house party. In terms of leadership, I had done very little apart from workshops and a weekend when I headed up the host team in fear and trepidation.

The day came when everything changed. Alan Smith, one of the chaplains who was to lead the house party came to me early in the morning looking very 'green' and said 'Sheila, I am so sorry but I am ill, you will have to take over!' I could not believe my ears. I had never led a week-long house party, leave alone a house full of young people in their twenties and thirties. Fortunately I had a brilliant young team who could not have been more supportive and it turned out to be a memorable week for guests, the team and not least me.

On the Tuesday morning seventy of the guests had to be in Ilfracombe, twenty miles away, to catch the boat to Lundy Island. Could I get them out of breakfast and into their cars? Only with the utmost difficulty. Eventually the house was quiet and I collapsed, (not literally) with an acute pain in my chest which I was sure was a heart attack. It went quickly and I realised it was a combination of panic, tension, anxiety and everything else you like to name. The best remedy seemed to be the Chapel and there I soon found the cause.

I do not think I ever had any ambition to be in leadership, never looked for it, never wanted it. As a physiotherapist it came my way through circumstances. Now here at Lee Abbey the pattern was continuing. As I prayed and laid the whole thing before the Lord, the problem became obvious. In a nutshell, I was quite happy to be second in command but with someone else taking the full responsibility of leadership.

This was quite a revelation and there seemed to be only one answer which, being a little faint-hearted, I found quite hard to accept. But I did eventually pray 'Lord if you call me into leadership in any way, at any time, in any direction, I will take the full responsibility knowing you will be my helper.'

The remainder of the house party went with a swing and from then on I led all kinds of conferences and house parties with a little more trust in the God who can even use chest pains to catch the attention of one of his children.

Lee Abbey and Canada

During my time at Lee Abbey I was still on the national team of Wholeness Through Christ and available for one or two courses a year. On one such course I was in casual conversation with Margaret Hogan a lady from Canada who, when she heard I had not been to her country, suggested I paid her a visit. It was an invitation too good to refuse and in the following year I went on the first of many trips to that beautiful country.

I arrived in Vancouver after having spent a week in Arizona seeing amongst other things the wonder of the Grand Canyon – my friends Mathew and Salma Colles had persuaded me that Phoenix was almost on the way to Vancouver!

Margaret and I took a trip through the Rockies. For me, on this first visit, it was an awe-inspiring experience, almost overwhelming: the splendour and majesty of the mountains, the beauty of the lakes and glaciers and the anticipation of seeing a bear or a moose. We were doubly blessed when the coach stopped and there beside the road was a bear with two cubs.

Apart from a great holiday, the whole visit was memorable for several reasons. First, for the birth of a new hobby brought about through the magnificence of the Rockies: a camera and a tape of pan pipe music. This was the origin of the slide presentation I mentioned earlier in relation to the sharing of gifts at Lee Abbey. Over the years this has continued to grow with additional readings, further sequences and taped music.

The second presentation set to music by Jenny Pike also originated on that first holiday. I was spending a few days in Vancouver and the friend with whom I was staying took me to a place she had not visited before called 'Fantasy Gardens.' It had been created by the Premier of British Columbia, a Dutchman who had been a bulb grower. As well as the windmill there were craft shops and cafés and a very beautiful garden full of colourful flowers. As we wandered and came to the far end of the garden we were aware of a large gap and what looked like an open book inside the entrance. The inscription read 'I am the way, the truth and the life.' To our surprise as we went round this 'biblical' garden we found sixteen life-size figures or groups of figures depicting the life of Christ from birth to resurrection. They were not only life-size but life-like and my immediate reaction was to take a photograph of each one having the vision for using them for meditation. This is just what happened. Back at Lee Abbey Jenny composed the music, Kath Roberts, a member of community, added readings and this presentation was shown on many occasions, not least on missions where it could be used to present the gospel in an unusual and unthreatening way. I still show it whenever I can.

This first visit was also memorable because Margaret Hogan with whom I stayed was a member of the Church whose Rector Alistair Petrie I knew through the Wholeness Through Christ Ministry. We went to his Church and the following year when he came to England he invited me to go out to Canada for three to six months. When I asked him why he said, 'To be in fellowship with the Church'. Surprise, surprise, what did that mean?

John Perry gave permission and his blessing for a three-month visit believing that I would take with me some of the ethos of Lee Abbey and bring back something of benefit from Canada. These were an amazing three months. I was based at Brentwood Anglican Chapel on the Saanich peninsular on Vancouver Island. This is an interesting church in that originally it was a school chapel with pews down either side. The main school building was destroyed by fire and was relocated further up the island. The chapel was then taken over by the Anglican Church.

When Alistair came out from Scotland to become rector, it was clear that the church had to grow or close. In 2001 it is still open! I found myself in a very mixed congregation; lots of families with children, teenagers, older couples, single people and the elderly who came from far and wide.

I stayed with Margaret and took my full part in the life of the church. I joined a lively intercession group seeking God's will and way and praying for the church in general. I helped with individual counselling, attended PCC meetings and joined the music group with my clarinet. There was not much I did not see or experience in all that was going on and I could not have been made more welcome.

There were about six or eight home groups (known as house churches) and my main contribution was to bring them together for a series of teachings, a rather scary exercise in a different culture. I do not think I was a great success. It actually reminded me of the time when I was asked to go, with a friend Pat Lebus, to lead a course of Lenten Bible studies in a church outside Cambridge. The Vicar did not think he was capable of doing them!

Pat and I felt extremely inept, but after a little advice and tuition from our Vicar we went. On this particular evening it was my turn to lead and the subject was the Cross. I can only say I returned home in the depths of depression knowing I had made a hash of it to say the least. I sat in front of the fire in my flat wallowing in self pity at my failure and picked up a book I was reading at the time. Believe it or not the words that stood out were 'God is not so concerned with your success as your obedience.' I have quoted those words to myself many times since that day!

Since Alistair had been in Brentwood Chapel he had been teaching about the Wholeness Through Christ Ministry and while I was in Canada and on every subsequent visit I was part of the British Team who came out to help with the early Canadian W.T.C. courses. An experience I knew would not have come my way had I not been on the spot. We met in various interesting places including an Island, a ranch and a convent. For me variety is truly the spice of life!

I so enjoyed the three months, making many new friends, seeing the beauty of a wonderful country and experiencing a different environment. It was also a real learning time and such a privilege to share in so much of the life of a Church which through all its heartaches and trials was committed to seeking God's plan and purpose.

Three more prolonged visits to Canada from Lee Abbey were certainly not in my plan for retirement. On these visits I stayed mainly with Pam Singer who lived much nearer the church than Margaret. For two years running my part was to be particularly involved with the training of house church leaders. This took a great deal of preparation and I was thankful to draw on Mike Edson's teaching at Lee Abbey and many other sources as well as my own experience of being in a very good house group for many years. It was a stretching and challenging venture for one who felt very green!

Brentwood Anglican Chapel,
Vancouver Island

One of the areas of ministry for which Alistair became increasingly in demand in Victoria was to pray round a house, a building or a church where it was thought that a negative influence such as freemasonry, some occult practice or particular happenings in the past were still affecting the life and growth of the place. Alistair Petrie would always take a small group of intercessors with him and I was included in this, another learning experience for me. In many ways this was an extension or enlargement on the Wholeness Through Christ ministry where instead of looking at the brokenness and negative influences in the past life of an individual this same principle applied to bring wholeness and healing to a house, a building or a church,

Each time I went to Canada my learning went a step further. In particular through various conferences, I heard that God was not only concerned with bringing healing and freedom to individual people and individual churches, but to whole cities and communities and this was actually happening around the world.

One conference stands out in my mind. Pam and I drove with Alistair (no longer a Rector but a conference speaker) and Marie, his wife, in a very comfortable Eurovan through the Rockies to Calgary. We were met there by Helen Thornton and her husband Errol, who as a cartographer was interested in mapping the history of cities and the land.

Alistair and Marie Petrie with Pam Singer

The 'Transformations Conference' was held in a vast modern church with every conceivable facility, very different to any church building we have in England. It was there we saw the video 'Transformations One.' This video relates the stories of four cities round the world, very different but all broken communities with acute problems in relation to alchohol, drugs, crime and occult practices. Each one had been transformed through the power of the Holy Spirit and united persistent prayer.

It is such an encouragement to realize that God really is on the move in so many parts of the world; all He needs is our co-operation. At the same conference I witnessed a very remarkable event. Amongst the church leaders there was an Aboriginal pastor, a member of the Blackfoot Tribe, living on a reserve about 40 miles from Calgary. It was a most moving moment when he called all the speakers and their wives on to the stage and forgave them for the way the white man had treated the First Nation people and asked forgiveness for the way they in turn had responded in violence and hatred. He then presented each one with a pair of moccasins made on his reserve.

At the end of the conference the speakers reciprocated, called the pastor, his family and the members of his church on to the stage, forgave and asked forgiveness for what the white man had done to the Indians. I think they were all given a book. As a finale, the Indian pastor was invited to celebrate communion and to pray individually for all those present.

The great privilege for our little party of six was an invitation to share the Thanksgiving Day meal with church members on the reserve. They were so welcoming and after the meal took us in to the church where they laid hands on us and prayed for us. I am now the proud possessor of a pair of real Indian moccasins.

Life was not all work, Vancouver Island and my favourite Salt Spring Island had much to offer of interest and beauty and my camera was often hard at work. It took three months to capture an eagle on camera and the pod of whales looked like specks of dust on the photograph. I did manage a close up of a tail. One of the most exciting trips was a cruise to Alaska with its mountains, glaciers and quaint towns, a memory which will remain with me for ever.

One year a group of us went to Mount St Helen, the scene of the devastating volcano of May 1980. This is now a National Park. It was like walking around some kind of moonscape with the strange shapes of dead trees and barrier rocks stretching for miles around. Every now and again one could see small shoots of green emerging through the ground heralding signs of a new life and hope.

Another year Alistair, who loved travelling and organizing trips, took five elderly ladies through six mountain ranges in order to visit Waterton Lake on the border of Montana which he sees as the nearest place to heaven on earth. It is certainly beautiful but to me the whole trip seemed like heaven on earth - unbelievable scenery for ten whole days.

On my way home from these visits I would spend a weekend visiting friends in Calgary, which is near Kananaskis country. One of the most memorable days of my Canadian visits was spent in this area of the Rockies when the mountains and pine trees were glittering with the sun shining on the first virgin snow of winter. My visits to Canada were so very special, but so were the returns to England and home. I well remember driving back along the coast road to Lynton on a quiet Sunday morning. The sun was shining and as I looked at the sea on one side and across to the lovely hills and valleys of Exmoor on the other, I remember saying to my driver, 'I have seen some of the most magnificent scenery in the world but this, though very different, is equally beautiful.'

Walking into Lee Abbey again after three months away was a unique experience. I have never felt so well and truly hugged and welcomed! I was back home with my community again to take up again the life I loved.

Lee Abbey - Moving On

Once a year at Lee Abbey I would see the warden about my future and discuss if it was right to continue as a member of the pastoral team. I trusted John Perry and then Mike Edson to be honest because it has always been important to me not to hang on to a job, a ministry or anything else when I should be moving on and letting go.

It was in 1992 before leaving for Canada that I asked the pastoral team to pray about my future when I was away. I found it hard to ask this but I knew in my heart of hearts that although not urgent there were small signs that 'the game old bird' was not quite so game as she used to be. Was it time to think about leaving? If so, when? I wanted it to be my decision but I needed the support and prayer of my team.

On return from Canada the team told me they had discussed what I had asked, could not make a decision for me, but one of the Chaplains felt I needed some guidance. He came up with the suggestion that I should consider leaving within the next two years which would give me plenty of time to think about it and prepare for the next move. This was so helpful and just what I wanted to hear, it confirmed my own thoughts that I should leave by the time I was seventy five in June 1994.

Sometimes it is more difficult to make a decision when you have absolute freedom to go anywhere in the world. I knew it was right to stay in England but 'Where Lord? What have you in mind? What is your purpose for me?'

I had a home in Cambridge and many friends there but after such a long time away the thought of going back seemed wrong. The flat which had been let to a variety of tenants for ten years no longer felt like home and anyway climbing up and down twenty eight stairs was impractical. So, where Lord?

First I considered two or three places in the West Country where I had friends but none of the ideas took root. Then my nephew Jonathan came into the picture. He and his wife Fran said they would love me to come and live near them in Birmingham where I could see more of them and their four children and at the same time they could keep an eye on me as I became more 'wrinkly'. I was very touched by this suggestion especially as there would be the added attraction of being near a lively church with one of my favourite Vicars!

Was this where the Lord was leading me? I was excited at the prospect, having been rather isolated from my family for some years. However, investigations to find suitable accommodation proved totally negative, it seemed Birmingham was not to be my future home. Often during my journeys to and from Lee Abbey I would stay with my friends Peter and Betty Sonley in Lechlade; Betty is my childhood friend, we first met on my third birthday.

Together we had visited Cirencester occasionally and as I thought of the kind of place where I would like to live, Cirencester seemed to fit the bill. An attractive town, not too big and not too small, good flat walking (an important criterion) but with beautiful Cotswold country all around. Central, accessible and only one-and-a-quarter hours from my nephew in Birmingham. I also realized that on the doorstep was the Harnhill Centre for Christian Healing which had so many links with Lee Abbey.

All this, together with the fact that I would be near Betty and Peter, caused me to visit an estate agent and enquire about retirement flats. To my surprise, there was not only a wide choice but there were some within my price range. We wandered around and came across quite an imposing block of flats called 'Barclay Court.' My immediate reaction was, 'I like the look of the building, I like the location, I like Cirencester, let's find out further details.'

Shortly after this original visit Diana Marle came as a guest to Lee Abbey. I discovered she lived in Cirencester in the adjoining complex to Barclay Court. She invited me to stay to look round and I walked into an empty flat and immediately felt at home. By a miracle five months later the flat was still available and having sold my flat in Cambridge I became the proud possessor of a new home which I know was God-given.

Of one thing I was absolutely certain, leaving Lee Abbey was going to be one of the most difficult 'goodbyes' of my life but I knew I had to face it head on and not run away as I had done in the past. I was to leave immediately after Easter in 1994. Some months before this I had written to Donald Cameron, the Director of Wholeness Through Christ, knowing it was time to resign as a member of the national team. Apart from accepting my resignation what he also had to say threw me into a flat spin but for that I shall be eternally grateful.

Donald's suggestion was that some weeks before I left I should get someone to pray with me and release me from Lee Abbey and my ministry there. This would be the beginning of the letting-go process and help me when I left and moved on to pastures new. I could hardly bear the thought, it seemed so premature but something within me, I believe the Holy Spirit, told me that Donald was right. So, one morning I sat and wrote down everything I could think of for which I was thankful during my twelve years – a thank-you letter to Jesus and a long one.

I then thought of all the things with which I had been involved, ministry, workshops, missions, leadership, teams, activities, . . . all of which would need to be handed back to the Lord, together with guests and community. I think forgiveness came in too for the many times I had got it wrong. While I was writing, the tears began to flow and I knew this was the beginning of an enormous bereavement.

The next step was to invite Debbie Plummer, one of the Chaplains, to my room to voice with her what I had written and in prayer lay it all at the foot of the cross. She then, in the name of Jesus and the power of the Holy Spirit prayed for my release. It was a very special time and certainly important for the future.

As the run-down began I remember two things quite vividly. The first when I suddenly found myself crying out 'Lord, I have missed my own home so much over these last years.' I had no idea I felt so deeply about this; it was as if those feelings did not need to be recognized or find expression until I could be excited at the prospect of a new home on the horizon, and I was excited.

The second remembrance came in the form of a chorus which I found myself singing day after day:

*Faithful one, so unchanging
Ageless one, you're my rock of peace
Lord of all, I depend on you
I call out to you again and again
I call out to you again and again
You are my rock in times of trouble
You lift me up when I fall down
All through the storm your love is the anchor
My hope is in you alone.

* "Faithful One" Brian Doerksen © 1989 Mercy/Vineyard Publishing

This song summed up and affirmed what I knew God was and who I needed him to be at the present time: a rock, an anchor. Also, the amazing realisation of how faithful and loving He had been over the past years and the assurance that He would not change in the future.

The main reason I felt it was time to move on from Lee Abbey was the fact that trays in the dining room were growing heavier, my legs declined to bounce on the dance floor and leading a family house party with fifty children began to tax my decreasing energies. Apart from this the constant goodbyes became increasingly difficult, guests in and out and numerous community members whom I had grown to love forever coming and going. Goodbyes were something of a ritual and of great importance as was going out for a meal with members of your team and then the meeting with the whole community.

The event I felt most nervous about concerned summing up in a short space of time what Lee Abbey had meant to me over the years and listening to observations about myself from the warden and anyone else who cared to speak. Fortunately community and humour are inseparable and I could only describe the evening as a glorious mixture of emotion and hilarity with a much-loved family. For both sides it was important to be serious yet lighten the occasion with humour. For my part it seemed a good time to share two embarrassing moments which happened in relation to Mike Edson, the warden.

The first occurred on a party night when the pastoral team were making fools of themselves in a rock and roll-cum-disco dance. My enthusiasm, on the small stage, got the better of me and caused Mike to retire with a cracked front tooth while I retired with a bleeding thumb!

I thought Mike was joking when he came to me while I was cleaning coffee cups after lunch and said quite casually, 'Sheila, you have flooded my office.' It was true! The entire floor looked like a paddling pool with water still coming through the newly decorated ceiling. I had left a tap dripping on some underwear soaking in the basin in my bathroom above. Fortunately Mike was going on holiday, by the time he came back in two weeks the office was dry!

My elected time for departure was immediately after Easter and I could not have chosen a better house party on which to end. There would be different ways of enacting some of the events but there were two which did not change, they were unique to Lee Abbey.

During the previous week two large wooden crosses were placed up on the hill overlooking the sea and in full view of the road below. On Good Friday the third cross was carried up by four people followed by the procession of guests and community walking in silence. It was put in place and a vigil maintained between 12.00-3.00 p.m. with appropriate readings at intervals. There was freedom to come and go or stay for the three hours. On Easter morning before breakfast the guests were invited to go out to Jenny's Leap where there was a shelter built into the rock. This was converted into a tomb filled with spring flowers and in a recess the empty shroud. Here young community would dramatise some of the events of that first resurrection morning before we all sang a resurrection hymn.

It was important for me to say farewell to guests, those present at the house party I saw as representative of the thousands I had met over the years. I was very touched by the gift of a Portmeirion table lamp which holds a place of honour in my sitting room and is a constant reminder of the many lovely people whom I met over the years.

On the morning of departure I was in a daze, finding it difficult to believe that this was me. Could it really be the last time in Chapel as a member of community or would I wake up and find it was a dream? I remember being prayed for with hands laid on me to be released and sent out to the next phase of life and then found myself spontaneously leading a surprised company out of the Chapel singing 'You shall go out with joy and be led forth in peace . . .' I do not think my feelings could be described as joyful at that precise moment but it was an appropriate song to sing knowing without a doubt I was doing the right thing at the right time and I only had to put my hand in the hand of God and walk out into the future in trust.

The final farewell came with the Traditional Leaving Circle when at the ringing of the outside bell all the members of community gathered in the back yard while the person leaving went round and said goodbye to each one in turn. I had dreaded the thought but it was easier than

The 'Leaving Circle' at Lee Abbey

expected partly because I had said the more personal farewells previously and partly because I was still in a benumbed state.

Looking back on the many times I had been part of the circle I realized it was often harder for those staying behind who were going to feel the gap created by the one who had left. I was fortunate in not having to drive away alone. Instead I was collected by Bob and Pat Purdon and taken to their home in Cornwall; as ex-members of community they knew what leaving was like.

As we drove away from the house, out of the estate and through the Valley of Rocks, I knew I had achieved what would have been impossible had God not taken me through that grieving process at Jenny's Leap and had Donald not given his wise counsel about releasing a few months ago. I had said goodbye properly. I was leaving behind some of the best years of my life but certain things quite rightly came away with me and will never be lost. In a nutshell, my personality came fully alive over those years in a way I had not known before, I became 'Me.'

The memory of seeing God bring new life and hope to countless hundreds of people, guests and community alike and the unique and special bonds of friendship that were made across the generation gap will continue.

Yes, it was goodbye to being an active member of the Lee Abbey community with all that involved but no one can take away my thankful heart for those years – all I want to say is 'Thank you Lord for your indescribable gift.'

A New Community

On April 11, 1994 my third retirement began. I moved into my new flat exhausted, grieving but excited. I was so fortunate that before I moved in Bob Purdon had spent two days decorating and David Pritchard the brother-in-law of one of the residents stepped in with his practical skills to assemble cupboards and put up shelves, you name it and he did it and has done ever since!

The first thing I had to do was to get my own house in order and begin adjusting to a very different lifestyle.It did not take long to face the first hurdle – housekeeping. I was on my own having to cater for all my bodily needs. I had not shopped or cooked for myself for ten years therefore my cupboards were empty; not even a jar of coffee! Tesco's supermarket scared the life out of me: rows and rows of sausages, sausages and more sausages, washing powders, washing liquids, bio' s non-bio' s; whatever do I choose?

It seemed these endless choices extended to every commodity in the supermarket. Up one aisle, down the next – I felt ill – bought a few things I did not need and ran out quickly! Fortunately my friend Janet Fickling was there just at the right time and came to my rescue, took me in hand, sat me down to make a list of essentials then steered me round the store. It took some time to come to terms with the enormous changes which had taken place since I last looked after myself, but in time Tesco's did not seem so large and forbidding and choices became easier.

As the weeks went by I revelled in having my own home again. It was lovely to be living with my own furniture once more and I began to be a little more clued-up on cooking and shopping, even entertaining occasionally. It was so good to have someone I knew living opposite. Diana Marle not only gave practical help in a day given to polishing the furniture which my tenants in Cambridge had neglected for years, but we also became very good friends. We shared interests and for me having her living opposite within waving distance gave me the sense of security I needed.

Here I was settling in my own home but once again in community; this seemed to be a recurring pattern in my life. From boarding school to hospital to Lee Abbey and now to one of a very different nature but a community nevertheless. Each resident at Barclay Court has his or her independence. They have their own front door but with opportunities for meeting together for events in the communal lounge.

I cannot fail to see God's hand in this latest move. I was thinking primarily of practical security and the availability of help if necessary. God could see that I needed an environment where people could become friends and not just faces that pass on the stairs. When I first arrived, there were distinct tensions between the two complexes: Barclay Court and Priory Mews. To put it mildly the community spirit was not in evidence. Thankfully it has all changed and I can only marvel at what has taken place over the past seven years to create a family atmosphere.

There are several reasons; new residents coming in who are ignorant of past feuds and the work of Chris Bloomer our warden who has a real gift of hospitality and humour which breaks down barriers. We now enjoy all kinds of activities together and arrange some form of entertainment in the lounge at least once a month to which all friends are invited. My slides with music come out at least once a year and it is good to continue to use them.

I believe there are two more significant reasons for the change in atmosphere. Quite soon after I arrived Chris the warden came to my flat one day and said, 'I don't know what to do, my husband Dave has got religion, he has always spent Sundays reading the newspapers but he has suddenly cancelled them and reads the Bible instead!' Fortunately Chris did know what to do, she went along to church with Dave, joined an Alpha Course to learn the basics of Christianity and 'got religion' herself!

Barclay Court, Cirencester

Around about the same time as this four or five of us decided to meet each week to pray for the residents in the two complexes and the events we have in the lounge together with general problems or needs. We know that God is at work in Barclay Court and Priory Mews. Spiritually I missed Lee Abbey so much, the worship and prayer times, discussion, teachings and the constant Christian fellowship. Suddenly I was transported from a spiritual hot house into the wilderness. I tried to have prayer times and found playing tapes helpful but it would only take one favourite chorus to evoke memories and tears, this of course was both healthy and healing.

Fortunately the Harnhill Centre for Christian Healing based in an old manor house in lovely gardens is three miles outside Cirencester. Harnhill was the dream child of Arthur Dodds, the then rector of Chedworth who on taking church groups down to Lee Abbey had the vision for a healing centre in the Cotswolds. The vision came into being fifteen years ago, when the manor was purchased from Robert and Mary Henly who for two years before they retired had felt that their home would be ideal for a Christian Centre.

Harnhill Centre for Christian Healing, near Cirencester

The house is run by an inner team of nine headed up by a warden, an Anglican Chaplain plus an outer team of around seventy who give varying amounts of time to help with counselling of individuals, prayer ministry at the healing services and all the various needs of administration, house, kitchen and garden. There is room for twelve to sixteen residential guests and courses are held week by week and at weekends for healing, teaching and training with day courses on all kinds of subjects relating to Christian healing. Teams also go out at the request of a church to teach about healing.

When I left Lee Abbey, I had practically no pre-conceived ideas of what the future would hold apart from the fact that I would in some way be involved at Harnhill. I had visited previously and spoken there and they had made it clear I would be welcome. I was very grateful to Hugh Kent, the warden at the time, who said, 'Sheila, we shall not ask you to do anything until you are ready.' This gave me the freedom to go to some of the services to receive rather than to give.

After a few months I felt I was 'ready' and became part of the outer team. I did not find it at all easy, there were so many similarities but it was not Lee Abbey and part of my heart was still in Devon. Having said that, from the beginning Harnhill was a lifeline, I was on the same wavelength and was so welcomed into the family. It has taken time but now I have no doubt it is where I belong. Very unexpectedly I have been asked back to Lee Abbey twice as a speaker in response to an SOS and around ten times as a pastoral helper but although I love being there and slot back so easily I am always happy to return home at the end of the week. Harnhill is very much a part of home.   I see my involvement there as part of God' s tapestry, in a gentler way he is still weaving in some of the things I was doing in past years:-The occasional prayer counselling with individuals, prayer ministry in services, greeting guests, serving teas, showing slides, the difference is that with reducing energies I have a choice, I can say 'NO!' One of the great bonuses is that I have made many new friends both single and married.

The more difficult adjustment was to the Church. Having been an evangelical all my Christian life with involvement in the charismatic movement and the different styles of worship experienced at Lee Abbey, it was not easy to fit in with the more formal worship of a High Church where congregational participation in terms of music was mainly limited to traditional hymns.

I remember the principal of Romsey House in Cambridge once saying, 'I wonder what it would have been like sitting next to Jesus in the synagogue?' I cannot help wondering what it was like for people sitting next to me in those early days at Cirencester Parish Church. I think they must have been treated not with the warmth of love of God or the Holy Spirit but with the hot air coming from me through my frustrations.

Seven years on I can say things are very different, encouraging changes have and are taking place in the church and there is a real sense of expectancy that God is on the move in Cirencester. Fortunately, God has also been on the move in me challenging my negative attitudes. For the first three or four years, apart from helping with Alpha Courses, I was a Sunday services pew sitter taking little or no part in the life of the church, therefore knowing few of the congregation. Latterly through the new ventures of being able to socialize and meet new people through coffee in church and the monthly charity lunches together with involvement in one or two groups and teaching events, at last I feel I belong.

I think this feeling of belonging has also been enhanced because I was able to bring some of the Lee Abbey humour to a parish party and I am now known not for my depth of spirituality but for being able to keep a straight face when acting the fool! I have even been stopped in the street and asked, 'How do you do it!' Humour is essential in church life! Although I may still have struggles, I now want to go to church and am content to be in the place to which I believe God has called me.

I have received so much in my Christian Life and I keep reminding myself of the importance of giving, especially in praying for 'the church' in Cirencester, my own patch where I live and the town with its people. I am not very good at it but I am trying my best. I hope too it is clear from my testimony that God has brought people into my life at the right time for various reasons. When my friend Diana died in 1998 she left a big hole but as always I found God fills holes with something or somebody different. In this case it was two people who came at the right time. There is Catherine Pither who lives round the corner from Barclay Court;

Parish Church of St. John the Baptist, Cirencester

together we shared much of the pain and anxiety of Diana's illness, and as a result we have become good friends and often meet for Christian activities or a theatre club event!

Another hole was filled when Wendy Hewett joined us at Barclay Court. She has not only become a good friend but has helped me fulfil a long held desire to play the piano. As I have not played since I was at school and Wendy is very adept, it says much for her patience and tolerance that she seems to enjoy playing along with my bumblings as much as I do. A real sign of friendship and we do have a lot of laughs, not least when at my 80th birthday celebrations we were part of the entertainment and performed some very simple duets! Sadly the clarinet has had to go but I get a great deal of pleasure playing in a recorder group mainly for fun, not performance.

For more important reasons than duets on the piano my eightieth birthday must have special mention. It was wonderful to have parties around the country which for me brought different areas of my life together. My immediate family came to Barclay Court and contributed greatly to the occasion by bringing together their various talents. Sadly my great-nephew Tom Stevens could not be there due to pressure of exams but the real gap was the absence of my brother, Michael, who had died two years previously. He and I had a special bond even though we led very different lives but I know he would have enjoyed the occasion. It is quite possible that without my eightieth birthday this book might never have come about.

The seeds were sown when a friend, Di Salkeld, took me out for a birthday lunch and started questioning me about my retirement activities and then suggested I should be writing them down. Certainly without her initiative and encouragement this story, which has been enlarged considerably along the way, would not have been written.

As I look back I can see how each phase of my life has been a preparation for the next. I can say from experience that God knows what is best for me and in his economy nothing is wasted. I have to say that although I never felt a specific call to singleness, I can now say with absolute assurance it has been God's best for me because 'Submission to the divine will is the softest pillow on which to recline' (from 'Streams in the Desert' compiled by Mrs Chas Cowman) and I have had wonderful experiences which I would never have had if I had been married.

If I only had a few words with which to describe my life from 1974 when I retired as a physiotherapist and 1994 when I retired from Lee Abbey, I think I would say, 'It was an incredible journey of discovery full of God given surprises.' If I only had a short sentence with which to describe the last seven years I would say 'It has been a journey of increasing contentment full of thankfulness to God for His generosity in giving me so much more than I expected in my third retirement.

I feel thankful that even through times of sadness and difficulty I have never had cause to doubt that God led me to the right place in which to live, thankful that after years of living to a timetable I now have the joy of increased leisure to visit and receive visits from my family and friends; thankful that I have the time to be creative and enjoy photography, art and music; thankful that I have the health and wealth to get on a plane and go to Malta – Crete – Canada; thankful that so much that I learned, created and enjoyed over the past years has been carried forward and continues to be used in various ways and in different situations.

Looking back with a bird's eye view of the whole journey two things emerge quite clearly, the first that all the way along I have had companions to travel with me, family, friends, counsellors, preachers who have loved me, prayed for me, taught me, listened to me, encouraged me and challenged me. God used each and every one to help me on the way. I can only say thank you: without you I would have fallen by the wayside.

Now the future is unknown in terms of health and strength but my certainty is that I have a faithful loving God who is not limited by my increasing age and declining strength. I believe my part is to trust, be thankful and live each day as fully as possible using as a bedrock two prayers which I have loved and prayed for many years.

I take God the Father to be my Lord,
I take God the Son to be my Saviour,
I take God the Holy Spirit to be my Sanctifier,
I take the word of God to be the rule of my life,
I take the people of God to be my people.
And now I commit myself – mind, body and spirit
To my Lord and Saviour Jesus Christ;
And I do this freely, fully and forever
In the name of the Father, and of the Son and of
the Holy Spirit.

Father God, take me today and use me as you will
through the words I speak, the things I do and
the prayers I pray and by your Holy Spirit bring
life to all those with whom I am in contact today.

My journey continues . . . One Way   Single   in faith.

My heartfelt thanks are due to so many people:

To **Di Salkeld** for insisting I should write this book and for making me sit down with a tape recorder to begin it.

To **Chris Fox** for her time and the skills in deciphering my handwriting and producing one draft after another with unfailing patience.

To **Ann Webb** who, from the beginning, read each draft and came back with her constructive comments. Without her I might well have given up.

To **Patsy Kettle,** who came in near the beginning and again towards the end and gave me her honest and positive comments.

To **Wendy Hewett** for her good work on the computer and for her unfailing interest whenever I have said: 'Please sit down and read this.'

To **St. Mary's Convent, Wantage** for the quiet of their guest wing and to **Sister Janet,** the guest sister who took such an interest in what I was doing.

To **Kate Wiggins** for her hospitality, for the hours spent in her dining room and for the shared Chinese take-aways.

To **John Perry** for his kindness and generosity in writing the Foreword.

To the author, **Brian Doerkson** and the copyright holders, for allowing me to reprint the words of 'Faithful One' on page 101.

To **Christian Brann** for his expertise, his honesty and for being so generous with his time. Without him there would have been no book. And to Mary Rose, his wife, who read and corrected the text again and again.

Last, but not least, a big thank-you to **my many friends** who have read what I have written, listened and, most important, prayed for it and to all those **married friends** who have made me feel **special as a single person.**

Sheila Stevens
Cirencester, November 2001